# Starting & Building an Awesome Nonprofit Organization for a New Generation

*For Founders, Executive Directors and Board Members*

## Simone Joye Eford

SimoneJoye.com | @SimoneJoyeEford

# STARTING & BUILDING AN AWESOME NONPROFIT ORGANIZATION FOR A NEW GENERATION

Copyright © 2017 by Simone Joye
Published by the Eford Group International LLC, New York, NY

Book and Cover design by Eford Group International LLC
ISBN 978-0-9995276-5-8
EBook ISBN 978-0-9995276-3-4
Published in the United States of America
First edition: December 2017
10 9 8 7 6 5 4 3 2 1

# ABOUT THE AUTHOR

*Simone Joye Eford* is a visionary, charismatic social entrepreneur and public speaker with a history of nonprofit leadership in New York, New Jersey and Georgia.

Simone is a million-dollar fundraiser, three-time executive director and the founder of two nonprofits—The National Association of Nonprofit Professionals (nanpp.org) and Young People Matter (YPM), an organization which provided emergency shelter and services to homeless, runaway and sexually-exploited young people in Atlanta.

As a nonprofit and media communications consultant, Simone has worked with a myriad of nonprofits, elected officials, entertainers and individuals including: PSE&G, Radio One Atlanta, Boys & Girls Clubs, the YWCA of Greater New York, along with the governments of Bermuda and Ghana.

Simone has also served as a board member of the National Association of Black Journalists (NABJ) and as an advisory board member of the Roddy White Foundation.

For her commitment to helping others she has received numerous awards and accolades including the:

- Humanitarian of the Year Award from the Southern Christian Leadership Conference (SCLC)
- Norman Borlaug/MedAssets Humanitarian Award
- US House of Representatives' Special Congressional Recognition by Congressman Hank Johnson
- Georgia Outstanding Citizen Award – Secretary of State
- Be Greater Award-United Way/SunTrust/Atlanta Hawks
- Thomas C. Wilson Youth Services Award-NAACP DeKalb
- Woman of the Year-Zeta Phi Beta Sorority
- Outstanding Print Journalist-Hunter College/CUNY
- Scholarship awards: NABJ and the New York Association of Black Journalists.

# DEDICATION

God first. Always. Thank you.

To my children, *A'shey* and *Chad*—the best young people I know. Thank you for your love and unselfishness in sharing your mom with the work that allows me to serve humanity. I Love You.

To my father, *Roney Eford, Sr.* who taught me the word "can't" should not exist in my vocabulary.

To the nonprofit professionals and clients who have hired me over the past twenty-five years, thank you for the opportunity to share your vision.

# ACKNOWLEDGEMENTS

To the Founders and Executive Directors who have inspired me.

*Diane Herbert*, Past Executive Director-SEBNC

*Milton Little*, CEO--United Way of Greater Atlanta

*Roxanne Spillett*, Past Executive Director and the first female to lead the Boys & Girls Club of America

*Geoffrey Canada*, Founder and Past CEO-Harlem Children's Zone

*Dawn Murray*, Founder--House of Dawn.org. Thank you for your unwavering support for a fellow nonprofit founder.

*Dr. Beverly Browning*, CSPR, Author of *Grant Writing for Dummies*. Thank you for being an inspiration for grant writers everywhere and for always taking my call.

You're among the best to ever do it!

# LET'S END YOUTH HOMELESSNESS

No child should ever have to sleep on the streets in America. Please support the nonprofits that provide havens for them.

# CONTENTS

# INTRODUCTION

*"Every master was once a beginner.*
*Every pro was once an amateur."*
*Robin S. Sharma*

As a nonprofit and media consultant, I converse with many individuals who possess a burning desire to start and build a viable nonprofit.

Their ideas are innovative, impactful and impressive.

They are going to save the world.

They are frustrated. They are tired of workshops and webinars.

They state the internet is filled with antiquated information. They always want to know how to obtain grant funding fast.

They have grown impatient waiting for their first paycheck in exchange for their hard labor and sacrifice.

Perhaps, you share those feelings as well.

I understand. I've been there myself a time or two as a nonprofit founder and a hired executive director with twenty-five years of working in the nonprofit sector.

Doing good for others should not be so hard right?

This book is written for the weary, the curious and the conquers. The founders, executive directors and board members of start-up and small-to-mid size nonprofits who serve the public good. In my opinion, you are among the best people in the world!

Starting and building a nonprofit is hard work. Faith may get you through the door, but it will not be enough to sustain a corporation. This book will assist you in balancing those dynamics that work for me and countless others every day.

We all have fumbled a time or two, so I cannot promise you 100% success. Real-life stories help us avoid common mistakes. Most of my clients hire me to help them get through the maze.

Many new nonprofits are started by people who work full-time jobs, so I have made the book succinct on purpose.

Finding the nonprofit "founder's story" is difficult. In the public space there is a plenitude of information on hired executive directors and the business of a nonprofit corporation.

What about the people, like yourself, who begin or are working in nonprofits from scratch?

Emphatically, the world needs more people like you.

Keep building, you are making society better for us all.

With Warm Regards,

*Simone Joye Eford*

*Please consider leaving a book review on the site where you obtained a copy.*

# CHAPTER 1
# Your Nonprofit Dream is Valid

*"No matter how hard the battle gets or no matter how many people don't believe in your dream. Never give up." Eric Thomas*

You are starting a nonprofit.

You are building a new venture.

You have a burning passion to help others.

You see a community need and you want to make a change.

You likely wake up each day with a great sense of purpose.

You're excited.

You want to inspire and motivate others.

You will change the world.

Congratulations!

*Here's what your life really looks like as a Founder/Executive Director:*

You will be tired. Very tired. Exhausted.

You will be frustrated. You will feel lonely.

You will sacrifice your family and friends.

You will use a lot of your own money.

People will discourage you.

People will borrow (steal) your ideas.

People will tell you your mission is short-sighted.

People will say you are taking a vow of poverty and you will be poor the rest of your life.

You will want to quit.

Don't.

Give yourself five minutes of self-pity each day, then go be the best nonprofit leader ever.

You are needed.

Although few will want to admit it, the nonprofit sector is a competitive business. Not shark like, but competitive nevertheless. Do not let that discourage you.

The spirit of collaboration hovers in our daily life. Yet, I am willing to bet there are only a handful who will admit how they snagged $50,000 from Corporation A or how they received that free space from School X.

You can do it too and this book shows you how.

## *How Do I Pay Myself as a Nonprofit Founder?*

That is the number one question nonprofit founders ask me. The other is, "How much do I pay myself?"

Fret not, you are not alone. Even experienced board members of larger nonprofits ponder over the compensation of their hired executive directors

Chapter Seven goes into the details where you will find information on start-up resources that pay salaries for founders and small nonprofit leaders.

# Starting & Building an Awesome Nonprofit Organization for a New Generation

Let's start with the number one reason almost anyone goes into business or gets up to go to work. To make money. Let's not fool ourselves.

Yes, you absolutely deserve a salary and benefits as the founder of a nonprofit.

The media's focus, on how much nonprofit employees make versus our for-profit counterparts, has guilted our industry into believing not only do we not deserve to earn a fair wage, but we should work for free. After all, while you are saving the world do you really need to pay your own bills?

According to the *Nonprofit Times*, the average salary for an executive director is from $60,000 per year to seven figures. Women still earn less than men (83 cents on the dollar) but we're working on that changing that.

It is noble to want to make a difference. It is not so exciting when you cannot pay your own bills. There is no hashtag called #brokeforacause.

You will not have to run a nonprofit without a salary. In fact, that should be one of your top priorities. If you cannot survive how will you help others?

In 2014, approximately 2,700 employees of tax-exempt organizations received annual compensations of more than $1 million dollars.[1] They are the CEOs of large national nonprofits such as United Way and hospitals. Their salaries, which many believe are excessive, are making legislators review federal tax exemption laws and have nonprofit lobbyists worried.

Will you ever get to a seven-figure salary anytime soon? I am not sure, but who is to say you cannot? Others have done it from scratch. The average nonprofit executive director does indeed earn six-figures in major cities. There are also a host of other perks which include housing and vehicle allowances.

Make no excuse for what you want to earn. Despite the critics, you can earn a decent income from working in and leading a nonprofit.

Most of the complaints about salaries are from nonprofit staff and watchdogs, not the upper leadership. There is a reason for that.

Your goal is to determine what salary you are comfortable with and when you can afford it.

What most seem to forget is that nonprofit executives work harder for their salaries than most for-profit and government employees. Yep, I said that.

Your hours will be long, and you will always believe there is something else to do. That is just something innate in nonprofit leadership. I think from the time we sign up for the work that changes the world our minds create the hashtag #staybusy.

Not enough credit is given to nonprofit leaders who work hard for every penny. I have easily worked 80 hours a week consistently for months in a row. I've earned six figures and I've also earned no figures. I have no complaints.

Few will understand the logic. Just as few may understand why you want to start a nonprofit in the first place.

# Starting & Building an Awesome Nonprofit Organization for a New Generation

I like to think of America as a capitalistic society with a heart for the less fortunate among us. But there are just some people who prefer profits over people. It is what it is.

That is why you should consider yourself a remarkable person. You are also among the crème de la crème of humanity. Your efforts will make someone else's life better. I want to believe the universe thinks that is priceless and good karma for you and your loved ones.

## *The Four Stages of a Nonprofit*

There are four major administrative/operational stages of a nonprofit.

- Seed Stage (Idea)
- Start-Up Stage (Implementation)
- Growth Stage (Securing Impact)
- Mature Stage (The Legacy)

In some manner this book will cover them all. It's important to remember what stage you are in because that is how funders will view you.

Each stage is meaningful.

Newer nonprofit leaders tend to jump from the seed stage to the growth stage too quickly.

Securing impact means providing program services and having the funding to match it. If you skip, or jump around, the stages it will throw things off balance. Other nonprofit professionals and funders will know.

Everyone except you who may wonder why you are working so hard but are progressing slowly.

Always remember what stage you are in and work accordingly. It will eliminate feeling overwhelmed and help you accomplish more. Nonprofit building is like a puzzle with many pieces. Methodically, step by step is how you grow.

## CHAPTER 2
# Failure is Not an Option

*"If there exists no possibility of failure,
then victory is meaningless." Robert H. Schuller*

Yes, I am putting this up front. In your face. On purpose. It is a terrible thing to see a good nonprofit fail.

It happened to me once after I quit my job and invested about $30,000 of my own money into starting one.

In my early 30s, I had this grandiose dream. I would create a nonprofit that would get a job for every unemployed young adult and underemployed woman in America's poorest Congressional District—the South Bronx.

That was my first mistake. The services were too broad. And as the saying goes, "I didn't have a pot to piss in or a window to through it out of."

All I knew is I wanted to assist people in a community where my late grandmother resided for over 40 years. They had the highest unemployment rate in the city. Let's get them a job so they can feed themselves and their families.

Even with threat of not being able to pay my own bills, I still rerouted my personal funds and paid the nonprofit's office rent. It was like gambling in a casino. Next month, it will get better. We will raise the money we need, or so I thought as we continue to help program participants with a smile and wishful thinking.

The reality hit me after the threat of a car repossession. I knew I had reached the end. My pockets were almost empty and ironically, I needed a job myself.

My ex-husband left employment applications on the dining room table with smiley faces. My family teased me. "You're the poorest adult in the family. Always ready to help someone else, now you need a loan," an aunt so eloquently relayed as she handed me a check for $5,000. Heavy sigh.

Our participants had to find other resources as we shut down after one year with approximately 140 people on a waiting list.

Where had I gone wrong? It gnawed at me. It kept me awake many nights.

Instead of giving up, I got another job in a nonprofit. It was time for me to learn the "business" side.

My new position was as the director of development and marketing at thirty-year-old nonprofit in that same neighborhood and a place I had attended summer camp as a child.

I was convinced I would make a difference. It was a mid-size agency with over 100 employees and a $10 million operating budget. I wanted to learn everything I could.

What I found out was, in the nonprofit I had created, we had an excellent program model, but the administrative and operational side was almost nonexistent. We were "program heavy."

# Starting & Building an Awesome Nonprofit Organization for a New Generation

I studied the executive director's job duties and shadowed his deputy director. I asked a ton of questions. I hovered over the fiscal and the human resources director. On lunch hours and breaks, I picked their brains. I volunteered to edit their policy manuals.

After I created a program and won a state grant, I was also assigned the new job of Program Director.

Essentially, I was educated on the job and paid my dues. I learned the job of an executive director. Prior to that I was just a founder of a program.

Four years after I began there, I left.

At the age of thirty-five, I found my dream job and was appointed the Executive Director of a Boys & Girls Club where my salary doubled to six figures.

All that administrative, operations and program experience was put to work fast.

I raised nearly $2 million dollars, increased the number of young people served by 30% and closed a $300,000 deficit all in my first six months.

Make no mistake, it was not easy. I wish I had a book like this back then. However, I proved to myself, what I had known all along. I could run and successfully operate my own nonprofit. I worked hard. It took me six years, but I eventually went on to open another nonprofit doing what I loved and helped thousands of young people and their families in the process.

## *Why New Nonprofits Fail*

**#1:**     Lack of your own financial support.

The reality is no one should go into business without their own capital. You should be the first investor. Even with a for-profit business a bank will require them to have collateral for a loan. I am in awe at the number of people who think "free money" flows to a nonprofit.

**#2:**     Failure to garner the support of the community you would like to serve.

**#3:**     Leaders have not created a viable business model. As a nonprofit leader/founder you must learn all the areas to make a nonprofit viable and sustainable prior to beginning.

**#4:**     Duplication of efforts—your idea is already being done or not needed. Why compete with the program already doing the work you want to do? Go and partner with them.

**#5:**     Attempting to provide services which are too broad in scope. Try and fill a "niche within a niche." For example, if you are opening an agency which will assist seniors, think outside of the box. Target seniors who also may be blind or who are homeless. Assist not only an immigrant who may need to learn English as a second language (ESL), but one who only speaks French.

**#6:**     Investing too much in program services while neglecting the administrative/operational structure. As a new nonprofit leader, you should dedicate at least fifty percent of your time to the managerial structure. The sooner you get it out of the way, the better. Do not rush to provide services until your management structure, which is detailed in this book, is solid.

If you fail to do so, you will encounter many interruptions while doing the work you are passionate about.

**#7:** New leaders lack nonprofit experience and need a nonprofit mentor or consultant.

**#8:** Treating a nonprofit as a private business.

## 17 Ways Not to Run a Nonprofit into the Ground

**#1:** **Be Frugal.**

Do not overspend. Every penny should be carefully spent. You will learn more later about nonprofit budgets which guide our world. You will want to save funds at every opportunity. Have you tried everything you can to find a cheaper office space? Do you really need supplies from an office supply store or can you shop at a dollar store?

**#2:** **Do Not Apply for Credit Too Soon.**

In a for-profit business, many entrepreneurs seek to obtain a bank loan, or a line of credit, to start their operations. In the nonprofit world, any debt will look sketchy when a grant funder reviews your financial reports. They may believe their financial donation will be used to pay that debt. .In addition, any debt may also adversely affect your nonprofit's DUNS report which is discussed in Chapter Four.

Wait until your nonprofit is viable and has enough resources before you apply for credit. Of course, that is not to say you should not apply for credit in your own name as a personal investment.

**#3:     Self-Learning Goes a Long Way.**

Investing in this book is a great example of self-learning. Whenever you can, learn how to do things on your own for independence and as a cost-saving measure. A simplistic example is your website.

For years, we spent tons of money on a "webmaster." With each new edit, I had to pay someone. Then one day, I decided to teach myself using Citymax.com. I also played around a bit with WordPress.com. After a few weeks, I was able to build our own professional website. That budget line was quickly deleted.

**#4:     Do Not Confuse Leadership with Ownership.**

Founders are not the nonprofit's owner. The founder/executive director's role is as the "manager" of resources. Although you are a small business, you should never think of yourself as a small business "owner."

**#5:     Do Not Depend on One Source of Revenue.**

This one I learned the hard way. Never put your eggs, or funding, in one basket. Diversified funding is a survival must for nonprofits. Funding changes each year and you should never believe you are guaranteed a renewal, especially with government funding. Chapter Nine provides viable and proven ways to accomplish this.

**#6:     Keep your Internal Processes current.**

Every so often our smart phone requires us to download updates. The same goes with the processes you will use in your office. From bookkeeping to grant writing, make sure you have established functions that are up-to-date and are familiar to most.

It is time consuming to find out that most of the nonprofit world may be using QuickBooks, but your agency uses some antiquated, or unpopular, system that only the bookkeeper, who just quit, knows.

### #7:    Be Mindful of Embezzlement.

People steal. People you hire will know you are new to the sector and the financial reporting. They may also think you are too busy to notice misappropriated funds. Your state's Attorney General's office is likely filled with open investigations regarding nonprofit theft. You, and your treasurer, should plan for tight fiscal controls and review your financials and bank statements on a regular basis.

### #8:    Always Have Excellent Representation

Your organization is your ID. Everyone who works, or volunteers, with you represents your nonprofit. Make sure they are of good character and are scandal-free.

### #9:    Plan for Disclosures to the Public.

As a nonprofit you are required to disclose certain information to the public upon request. It is similar to the Open Records Request Act for government entities.[2] If you fail to comply and someone notifies the IRS, you may warrant an investigation and/or an audit of your organization. Prepare a plan early for such requests.

**#10:    Do Not Hire Unqualified Friends or Family.**

No matter what, avoid hiring (or adding them to your board) any unqualified friends and family. There will be a few who may beg you for a job. It's a big mistake. Across the board every person should go through the same hiring and vetting process. They should apply for open positions like any other candidate. They should submit their resume and have formal interviews. A member of your board should also interview them.

If they are not qualified do not hire them. If hired, make sure they report to someone other than you. I could fill up an entire chapter on the mistakes of hiring family and friends, or having them serve as board members, that would make your head spin.

**#11:    Take Care of the People Who Help You.**

Staff turnover is a huge issue in the nonprofit sector. Please and thank you still goes a long way, along with days off with pay (like a Friday before a long holiday weekend).

One of the largest complaints of nonprofit employees is the lack of earning livable wages. Whenever you can, pay people what they are worth.

Do not be too cheap in this area, as you will likely expect a great deal from your staff. It's a different story if the funds are simply not there. However, you should know your staff can easily find out if you are jerking them with wages.

If you do not have the funds, think about utilizing flex-time in your office. Offer perks which can include paying for their professional development workshops/classes. Try and remember their birthdays. If you can set up a staff lounge area with complimentary snacks and beverages.

Refrain from being petty with time (e.g. lateness), so when you need employees to work extra hours they will not resent it. Think of other ways you would like to be rewarded by an employer for your hard work and use it for your own attrition.

### #12:    Avoid Burnout.

Stress, anxiety and exhaustion are a way of life in the nonprofit sector. Some get used to it, others breakdown. It can kill morale.

In your office, try and create a good work-life balance. Try and team up your staff with a volunteer (or an intern) who can assist them for a few hours a week (or on a per project basis). Volunteers are not just for special events or one-day projects. Utilize their services to help you and your team.

### #13:    Don't Chase the Money.

Always put your mission over money. There is a lot of funding out there for worthy causes. Make sure you only apply for the ones which are in alignment with your mission. Many nonprofit leaders look for open grant opportunities and then create services to fit them. A potential funder will thoroughly research your work. They will quickly notice if you have tried this strategy and even the best written grant application will likely be rejected. You also risk being blacklisted from that funding source for "chasing the money."

### #14:    Focus on What's Right Instead of What's Wrong.

Funders already know the problems. You want to be the nonprofit that tells the world how your work is making things better. In the past, "the need" was critical. That is not the case today. In federal grant applications, it still is a big section to answer, but not as large as the impact area.

Today, "impact," "transformational impact," "outcomes" and "evaluation" of your services are more important than ever. Be prepared to collect data to measure your lasting impact.

Are you keeping attendance sheets? Do you have a system for getting the opinions of program participants, via surveys? What are you doing to change the problem? These are some examples of how to gauge your impact.

## #15: Partner/Collaborate with Others

How do funders think? Collaboration, collaboration, collaboration. No nonprofit is an island. You will not be successful working alone. Ever.

There are many ways to partner with others. The simplest? Just ask especially when they are needed for a grant you are seeking.

If you do not yet have a formal working relationship with other service providers, you can easily create a referral network for program participants.

For example, if you are a basketball club, connect with organizations that may offer free SAT prep to the kids you serve. If you work with women returning to the workforce, partner with an organization which may provide them with free resume creation.

Now you have organizations to add to your referral network and they will likely do the same.

### #16: Create a Strategic Plan.

Every nonprofit should have a strategic plan, which includes your fundraising goals. This is your roadmap to success. It should be crafted in two to five-year intervals.

### #17: Do Not Stay Quiet or Hidden.

Never miss an opportunity to broadcast your success. Tell your story. And then tell it again.

Have you received a new financial donation? Tweet about it.

Have you received a government grant which is expected to help 1,000 people get into housing? Send out a press release.

Did your elected official donate? Take a picture and share.

Have you convinced a notable person to join your board? Post it on Facebook. You helped save someone's life and they are willing to share their story with the world? Post their picture & story on Instagram and then email Gayle King of *CBS This Morning*.

I think you get the point which is really, do not be shy or quiet. The more people know who and what you do, the more you will garner support.

You can use other marketing options provided in Chapter Seven to help bring out your creative juices.

# CHAPTER 3
# Today's Nonprofit Industry

*"Change before you have to." Jack Welch*

The nonprofit sector is an excellent industry to begin a new business. There are nearly 1.5 million tax-exempt nonprofits in the United States. Together they represent $3.4 trillion dollars of the US economy.

The nonprofit sector employs nearly 11 million workers, which is roughly 10.3 percent of the US total workforce.

When I began in the nonprofit sector in the early 1990s we researched grants by spending a day at the Foundation Center (foundationcenter.org) or we bought their huge directory of funding prospects. You could easily spend an entire day searching for sources. To apply for grants, you had to use postal mail.

Now you can purchase a Foundation Center license for access to their online directory which consists of 140,000 U.S. foundations.

Funding software was limited and difficult to navigate. We kept DOS-based donor lists. When I first learned about Raiser's Edge, which is the father of donor management systems, I was in heaven. Twenty-five years later, they still provide a great system for organizing your donors.

# Starting & Building an Awesome Nonprofit Organization for a New Generation

Technology has made it easier, faster and more effective to apply for funding. Take advantage, every day.

As I can recall, the New School for Social Research, located in New York City, was the first college to offer a class on nonprofits. When I found out, I would dream of teaching there.

Today, thousands of schools offer nonprofit courses at the undergraduate, graduate and doctoral levels which can be done online. Perhaps looking around their website at the courses would not hurt you as a new nonprofit leader. You should become well-versed in the world of nonprofits outside of "programs" and "grants."

I also remember when there were only a handful of national conferences for nonprofit employees which were segmented by areas of specialization (development, fiscal, etc.).

Today, the National Association of Nonprofit Professionals (nanpp.org) conducts a yearly conference for all nonprofit employees to convene. Make sure you're represented as it can bring you many benefits. The educational opportunities are priceless. You will also have an opportunity to network with your peers, gain allies, encounter new vendors who cater to nonprofits, and position yourself as an nonprofit expert.

In addition, a few days of "professional recess" away from the office may just what you need at least once a year.

## *Aging Out Leadership*

The nonprofit sector is experiencing an exodus of leadership. Executive directors are retiring in large numbers. The *Boston Globe* reports in *Nonprofits Hungry for New Leadership*,[3] "The expected exit of large numbers of veteran nonprofit executives, many of them baby boomers who shaped the charitable sector and whose departures create the risk of a widespread leadership vacuum."

Nonprofit leaders, including board members, have found they have not created adequate succession plans for new leadership. Founders are realizing they have not groomed anyone to carry on their legacy and are working longer than they really desire. Board members are also now older and are also aging out.

Ironically, the nonprofit sector fails to reach back for their own leadership patterns. Each year, some of the nation's largest corporations are on college campuses recruiting young people. Not so much nonprofit leaders.

According to the *2017 Nonprofit Employment Practices Survey*, a report from Nonprofit HR, more than half of the nonprofit sector lacks a formal procedure in place to recruit top talent.

You must think ahead so you are not one of them. Whether current leaders want to keep up or not, this change is opening the door to a new generation of social entrepreneurs who think and work differently.

# Starting & Building an Awesome Nonprofit Organization for a New Generation

Nonprofits must affect meaningful change to coincide with the way the world is rapidly changing. Believe it or not, there are some nonprofit leaders who are terrified at tweeting.

A new nonprofit leader must think like a new leader to survive and flourish with a business which is unique and impactful.

## *Gender Diversity*

The lack of gender equity within the nonprofit sector makes for an interesting conversation piece.

Women are the dominant employees with the nonprofit sector. We make up 75 percent of nonprofit workers and volunteers. Women are ahead on the front lines and outpace for-profit companies with the number of women in leadership.

Yet, most nonprofit boards are led by men. When it comes to the top nonprofit spot, such as the executive director/CEO, the number of women leaders drops to less than half (45 percent).

Women also earn 25% less than our male counterparts. NonprofitHR.org reports some interesting data about our younger generations:

"Millennial women nonprofit leaders are faring slightly better [than their male counterparts] earning 83 cents on the dollar, but Xer and Baby Boomer women leaders continue to lag behind their male colleagues. Come on, really? It's 2017."

My thoughts exactly.

No disrespect to my male nonprofit leaders, but if you are a woman starting a nonprofit, rock on sis! Rock on!

## *Racial and Ethnic Diversity*

Diversity within the nonprofit sector is dismal.

The Building Movement Project, recently released a comprehensive, eyebrow raising report entitled, *Race to Lead: Confronting the Racial Leadership Gap* (racetolead.org). The report cites, "The percentage of people of color in executive director/CEO roles has remained under 20 percent for the last 15 years." In addition, "Eighty percent of people across race think the lack of racial diversity at the top is a problem in the nonprofit sector."

Reality check here. Most nonprofit board leadership consists of those who are very wealthy and very White.

BoardSource.org surveyed over 1,750 executives within the nonprofit sector. They found: 90 percent of all nonprofit CEOs are White and 84% of board members are White.

The racial bias is disheartening. Not nearly enough of nonprofit leaders represent the diverse cultures and communities they serve.

Dare I say, this is an interruption in organizational performance? Many of the people who receive services from nonprofit organizations represent the diverse racial make-up of our nation. People of color are mainly found leading programs.

For example, Covenant House.org, which is one of my favorite charities, provides services to homeless and trafficked youth—an overwhelmingly number of them are young people of color.

Covenant House lists eleven executives on their website. Five of them, including the CEO Kevin M. Ryan, are White men. There are no Black, Latino, or Asian men in the senior leadership. There are five White women whose titles are "senior" vice presidents. There is one Black woman. Her position is "executive" vice president for program operations. A seemingly lower rank than senior VP and the only title of its kind.

Covenant House has 28 board members. Twenty-four of them are White and includes seven women. Three of them are Black women. There is one Black man. Four people of color in total. There are no Latinos or Asians.

Over ninety percent of the young people on their website are Black and Latino. It is not far-fetched to question their impact upon the young people they serve. Or to ask whether are doing themselves a disservice. Could they be reaching more youth or even, a larger funding base if they had more people of color at the helm?

I point out this dynamic because it is like this across the board in the nonprofit sector. I use Covenant House as an example not to attack them. I have submitted more resumes to work there as an executive than I can count. I love their mission. I am passionate about any organization that helps runaway youth. They are being used because even as one of the most revered nonprofits in our nation, they to still has a way to go in racial and ethnic diversity.

The irony is Covenant House may just be doing a better job than other national nonprofits—many of whom who have zero people of color, or women, at the helm of leadership.

Each day, the Facebook group, NPOCunicorns – People of Color Nonprofit Professionals, which has over 1,000 members, discusses diversity, racism and sexism in the nonprofit workplace. The stories shared are enlightening and worth a look. You may be able to add your own experience to the conversation. I love to visit because it lets me know I am not alone in the struggle for racial and ethnic equity in the sector.

Just as women rallied (and some argue are still rallying) for the shattering of the corporate glass ceiling, today we are going through a similar dynamic in the nonprofit sector. The lack of diverse leadership may threaten the future survival of many organizations.

The current nonprofit leadership across our nation must do more for inclusion and stop making excuses that they cannot find suitable qualified candidates. Is that really the case? You will need to learn strategies to work around them for your ultimate success.

A great example of what can be done is evidenced by the Toronto Chapter of the Association of Fundraising Professionals (AFP) who are leading the charge for those who raise money for nonprofits.

They have created an eight-month program, "A Fellowship in Inclusion and Philanthropy." The program is working, "To build a pipeline of fundraising leaders that reflect the diversity of our communities." If Canada can do it, so can we in the United States. I am thinking their program could potentially be modeled across all spectrums of the nonprofit sector.

# Starting & Building an Awesome Nonprofit Organization for a New Generation

## *The Mentor Effect*

Since you are starting (or building) a nonprofit, you should get a mentor.

That's exactly what I did in the early 1990s, after I left journalism to work full-time in the nonprofit sector.

My self-appointed mentor's name was Reda Edelstein. She worked as the Deputy Executive Director for Development at the YWCA of Greater New York. She was an avid fundraiser.

Each year 300+corporate male CEOs opened their checkbooks to outbid one another for a seat on the largest dais in the country. They bragged that they were among the best men in the country who were helping women advance up the corporate ladder in their Fortune 500 led companies. It was a competition based upon testosterone.

It worked. Reda's creative genius raised $2 million dollars for a three-hour luncheon at the Hilton, every year for years.

Working for Reda was my first real nonprofit job and working with a special events team. I started at the top of special events, not at the bottom. As such, it has been easy for me to put together revenue-building events.

Reda was a petite Jewish woman who was old enough to be my mother at the time. She lived with her wife and adopted Asian son in the progressive area of Park Slope, Brooklyn.

As a new nonprofit leader, you should know Jewish people are among the largest philanthropists in the nation and head an overwhelmingly amount of foundations.

Reda saw my eagerness to be a part of her 20-person development team. As one of the few Blacks on her staff, she bluntly let me know the world of philanthropy was about one color: green.

"If you can help us get more, I don't care if you are purple," she announced after I questioned whether I was the best person to request a $25,000 donation from an elderly White woman. The reality was I was nervous and lacked confidence. I felt race permeated everything in America, even donors.

"Does it matter to you if she is White?" Reda asked curiously. I felt embarrassed I had even bought up race.

I did my job and received that donation. More importantly, it set the stage for future requests and I was never nervous again.

I am not sure whatever happened to Reda, who is likely in her 80s by now if she is still with us on earth. I regret not keeping in touch.

She gave me the opportunity to work along some of the greatest fundraising minds I have ever met. That initial experience laid the foundation for a stellar career. There has not been one area of development and fundraising I have not excelled in. I believe it was because I had a phenomenal mentor.

Due to my ability to raise money is also a reason why I believe I was able to soar to the highest levels of the nonprofit sector.

That should also be your attitude. Looking for opportunities from those who truly know what the nonprofit sector is all about. Raising money, thinking about connections, and thanking others should be your way of life as a nonprofit leader.

# Starting & Building an Awesome Nonprofit Organization for a New Generation

Were it not for Reda, I probably would have quit the nonprofit sector and became a Pulitzer Prize winning financial editor. This book might have been about purchasing Bitcoins instead of starting and growing a nonprofit. Maybe in my next life. This time around, I choose to serve humanity without regret.

The point is, if you are a person of color, you just may be the only one at the table or in the room of nonprofit executive-level circles. If you are Black man you may find it difficult to find your counterparts. Do not be surprised. Do not let it stifle what you are trying to accomplish. It may seem more challenging to raise money, but I do not believe it will be because of race.

Some may call me naïve, or say I was a token. Could I have possibly raised more if I was White? Who knows, but millions are millions. Racism within the nonprofit sector is not as blatant as in corporate America. Most are progressive, forward thinking individuals, or at least this is what I would like to believe.

Look at the phenomenal story of Geoffrey Canada, the founder and past CEO of the Harlem Children's Zone (HCZ). Mr. Canada, an African American from the South Bronx, has built a nonprofit empire, raising millions of dollars from zero, despite, the lack of initial support and belief in his vision.

When I first met Mr. Canada, I was about 22 years old and still in college. His office was above a Chinese restaurant in three small rooms on a busy avenue in upper Manhattan. He was just starting HCZ and I was there to interview for a grant writer position.

During our three-hour long conversation, I remember thinking about the smell of the food wafting into the office. I thought I can't work here. I felt he had a long way to go.

What I also recall was his passion. He let me know he would not be in that space forever. I remember him telling me he was going through a divorce. He was starting over and was going to build the best nonprofit Harlem had ever seen.

Ultimately, I accepted the position with Reda the YW, but I am thankful for the conversation. It was that conversation that sparked my interest in starting my own nonprofit someday. He was the first "founder" I had ever met.

Although I believed in his vision and I have deep family ties in the Harlem community, I chose an established development department and the opportunity to work with a national nonprofit brand.

Today, although Mr. Canada is retired, the HCZ has annual revenues of over $100 million dollars. What's even more impressive is HCZ is one of the few nonprofits which has reached "platinum" nonprofit status (revenues of over $50 million dollars).

Mr. Canada's tenaciousness should be used as the inspiration, especially to new founders. You can Google him and listen to how he has accomplished so much.

### Inclusion includes Everyone

The new nonprofit must change the way in which we see people. Today, that is particularly important in the way we provide services and collect demographic data. When you purchase a donor management system, make sure you have options.

For example, we need databases which include Mx, a honorific used by nonbinary people and pronouns to describe people who do not consider themselves a he or she.

We still have a long way to go for gender and racial equity within the nonprofit sector. Do not let that deter you.

We are on the right road for nonprofit leaders and funders who are now realizing leaders must truly represent the diverse racial and ethnic makeup of the communities they serve. Perhaps, by starting and building your nonprofit, you will be contributing to that inevitable change.

## *Young Leaders*

Rising leaders are important to the nonprofit sector. I am an intergenerational thinker. If you are like me, old enough to have an AARP card, you should know there is no way you can compete with the energy of a millennial.

Working in nonprofit leadership means burning the midnight oil. The day after I am up all night, perhaps writing a grant, I am grumpy and tired.

Besides the energy level, members of a new generation work differently. Even work spaces today are different. At least 70 percent of US offices now have open worksites. That's up 64 percent more than the 1990s.

Years ago, a communal set-up without doors and windows to separate colleagues was called a staff meeting. After we finished, we all went our separate ways to our private offices.

Millennials seem to loathe the confinement. I mean who wants to sit alone in their own office with their head in a smart phone, when you can do it out in the open? Of course, that is a joke and I'm being facetious.

Having your own office used to be a huge perk in a nonprofit where space is often limited.

Today, getting out of one seems to be more beneficial as young people work in teams. You should remember this as you seek to obtain and design your own space.

Oddly enough, this new type of work synergy is exactly what is needed with the nonprofit sector. This type of work environment seems in perfect alignment with the spirit of nonprofit sector.

You will not be around forever. Put young people on your board of directors, promote them to managerial levels and make them a part of your sustainability planning. Without a shadow of a doubt, in the least, they should oversee all your social media communications—which is an important part of their lives.

## Working Remotely

Welcome to the 21st Century. Thanks to technology, you can now work from anywhere on the planet and stay connected to your colleagues. It is wise for nonprofit employers to offer telecommuting as an option. Let's keep as many carbons out of the air as possible, shall we?

Working remotely has worked for our teams in the past. The results were impressive. It assisted us with employee retention, lowered our overhead (electricity bills add up), and even saved on our water usage. Offering an option to work remotely is a great way to attract talent, including retired nonprofit executives.

When I have recommended this wonderful work experience to veteran nonprofit leaders, they shot it down.

"Working from home is a privilege and my staff has to earn it," one relayed while trying to figure out how to reduce his high staff turnover rate.

Another relayed, "I do not believe they will actually work if they do not show up in the office. I'm not paying people to be home."

My thoughts? If you cannot trust an employee will work from home, you should not trust they will work in your office either.

Remember the wise words of Sam Walton, "We are all working together, that's the secret."

# CHAPTER 4
# Dream It. Do It. Getting Started.

*"The fruit of your own hard work is the sweetest."*
*Deepika Padukone*

### *Are You Ready to Lead a Nonprofit Corporation?*

In my experience, most people who I have come across who would like to begin a nonprofit are "program" oriented.

They want to provide services at the very beginning. They believe to get started they can obtain "free" grant money.

If you find you share the same nonprofit ideology, you may want to ask yourself an important question. "Am I truly ready to lead a corporation? Or am I more comfortable with running a program?

For this book's purpose, it is written for those who are ready to be a founder/executive director/CEO, a title I am using interchangeably.

If you prefer to run a program, I recommend a fiscal sponsor/agent until you decide whether leading a nonprofit is really something you want to invest time, money and resources in.

## *Fiscal Agent/Sponsor*

A fiscal agent/sponsor is an organization that allows you to use their tax-exempt status to obtain financial donations. They also manage the funds as a sponsor.

You might find a fiscal sponsor/agent useful if:

1. You have a great program, but want to avoid the expense and time of creating your own nonprofit tax-exempt organization.
2. You can seek your own funding (e.g., write grants and other appeals)
3. You have a program which has not yet proven long-term viability.
4. You are awaiting your tax-exempt status from the IRS and would like to begin to solicit funding.

## *Pros of a fiscal sponsor:*

- Helps you qualify for grant funding quicker.
- They will receive and process grant funds for you.
- They will distribute your funds through their organization's account.
- You have formed a viable partnership relationship with another nonprofit.

## *Cons of a fiscal sponsor:*

- They have your donor list and will likely compete for the same funding.
- The sponsor has complete control and discretion over the funds. They must also legally ensure the funds are being spent correctly, so they may require written reports.
- If you do not have the proper written agreement in place, the sponsorship relationship may not exist according the IRS. If funds are given to you without the tax-exempt status being properly in place, the donation could be revoked by law, and the fiscal sponsor could lose their tax-exempt status.
- Although rare, the organization could take your program idea and use it as its own.

If you feel you need a sponsor/agent you can search for one at the Fiscal Sponsor Directory.org.

## *Out of Pocket: Your Personal Nonprofit Investment*

To open any business, you need your own investment. If you were opening a restaurant you would need your own capital to get started. It's the same with a nonprofit. It surprises me when I ask someone how much they have on hand to invest, only to hear, "We don't have any money; Can't we apply for grants?"

# Starting & Building an Awesome Nonprofit Organization for a New Generation

You certainly do not need a million dollars to start a nonprofit. However, you should have personal funds and other resources you can leverage before you take the leap into starting your own. Then think of the best way to use your resources. You have already invested a few dollars to purchase this book. Now, what else will you need offhand?

Think about a few preliminary costs:

- State incorporation filing fee;
- IRS fee for tax-exemption.
- State charity filing fee (if applicable)
- Bank deposit to open your account;
- Purchase of business cards and other marketing materials.
- Domain and website purchases.
- Internet service.
- Telephone (You can get a free telephone number with Google Voice with a Gmail account).
- Office rent, etc.

## *The Freebies: In-Kind Donations*

Start applying to organizations which provide donated resources to nonprofits. These are two of my favorites.

**#1:** If you love technology, **TechSoup.org** has it all. They provide nonprofits with heavily discounted software and hardware.

**#2: Good360.org**, formerly known as Gifts-In-Kind provides nonprofits with products, goods donated from the private sector. They boast the delivery of more than $400 million dollars in donated goods. Impressive. Companies such as HP, Walmart, 3M, are donors. See if you can find some donations to help your mission.

### Keep Your Receipts

Remember to keep every receipt, no matter how small. You should also keep records of your donations to the nonprofit. At tax time you can claim them on your personal tax returns.

Also keep track of your mileage. The IRS allows mileage reimbursement at 53.5 cents per mile for business purposes. If you are moving, it's 17 cents per mile.

### Draft Your Nonprofit Business Plan

They say behind every great business is a well, thought-out business plan. Most business plan samples you may find are geared towards for-profit businesses where the focus is on consumers and financial rewards.

A nonprofit business plan is slightly different. The bottom line are services and the way most of the revenue is obtained.

Draft a plan to use as your nonprofit roadmap.

The Small Business Administration (SBA.gov) has great information on creating a business plan. You can use their resources as an outline.

# Starting & Building an Awesome Nonprofit Organization for a New Generation

## Just Like This: The Top 15 Things to Do First

**#1:     Determine your tax exemption category.**

Make sure you qualify as a 501c3 nonprofit by reviewing the following chart. Not all nonprofits qualify as tax-exempt. You want to make sure yours will be a 501(c)3 before you apply.

The chart on the next few pages shows the different status for organizations.  IRS Publication 557, *Tax-Exempt Status for Your Organization* provides more details and updates.

| | |
|---|---|
| 501(c)(1) | Corporations Organized under Act of Congress (including Federal Credit Unions) |
| 501(c)(2) | Title Holding Corporations |
| **501(c)(3)** | **Religious, Educational, Charitable, Scientific, Literary, Testing for Public Safety, to Foster National or International Amateur Sports Competition, or Prevention of Cruelty to Children or Animals Organizations** |
| 501(c)(4) | Civic Leagues, Social Welfare Organizations, and Local Associations of Employees |
| 501(c)(5) | Labor, Agricultural, and Horticultural Orgs. |
| 501(c)(6) | Business Leagues, Chambers of Commerce, Real Estate Boards, etc. |
| 501(c)(7) | Social and Recreational Clubs |
| 501(c)(8) | Fraternal Beneficiary Societies |
| 501(c)(9) | Voluntary Employees Beneficiary Assoc. |
| 501(c)(10) | Domestic Fraternal Societies and Assoc. |
| 501(c)(11) | Teachers' Retirement Fund Associations |
| 501(c)(12) | Benevolent Life Insurance Associations, Mutual Ditch or Irrigation Companies, Mutual or Cooperative Telephone Co. etc. |

| 501(c)(13) | Cemetery Companies |
|---|---|
| 501(c)(14) | State-Chartered Credit Unions, Mutual Reserve Funds |
| 501(c)(15) | Mutual Insurance Companies |
| 501(c)(16) | Cooperative to Finance Crop Operations |
| 501(c)(17) | Unemployment Benefit Trusts |
| 501(c)(18) | Employee Funded Pension Trust |
| 501(c)(19) | Post or Organization of Past or Present Members of the Armed Forces |
| 501(c)(20) | Group Legal Services Plan Organization |
| 501(c)(21) | Black Lung Trusts |
| 501(c)(22) | Withdrawal Liability Payment Fund |
| 501(c)(23) | Veterans' Organization (created b4 1880) |
| 501(c)(24) | Section 4049 ERISA Trusts |
| 501(c)(25) | Title Holding Corporations or Trusts |
| 501(c)(26) | State-Sponsored Org providing Health Coverage for High-Risk Individuals |
| 501(c)(27) | State-Sponsored Workers' Compensation Reinsurance Organization |
| 501(c)(28) | Railroad Retirement Investment Trust |
| 501(c)(29) | Co-Op health insurance issuers |
| 501(d) | Religious and Apostolic Associations where members live in a communal life |
| 501(e) | Cooperative Hospital Service Organizations |
| 501(f) | Cooperative Service Organizations of Operating Educational Organizations |
| 501(j) | Amateur sports organizations |
| 501(k) | Child Care Organizations |
| 501(n) Charitable Risk Pools | Pools certain insurance risks of sec. 501(c) (3) organizations |
| 501(q) Credit Counseling | Credit counseling services |

| 521(a) Farmers' Associations | Cooperative marketing and purchasing for agricultural procedures |
|---|---|
| 527 Political Organizations | Contributions or makes expenditures for political campaign |
| 528 | Homeowner associations, condominium management, timeshare associations |
| 529 | Qualified tuition plans operated by a state or educational institution |

## #2:    Who Are You?

It's time to put away that resume. Entrepreneurs make biographies, aka a "bio."

You will need to construct one. Check the websites of other nonprofit executives you admire to craft your own. You can use mines in the Author's information section.

In your bio, make sure you focus the professional experience which is in direct alignment with the services you want to provide. Highlight what makes you the best person to lead your organization. Include your education, relevant volunteer experience and any awards, media coverage, etc. Some like to add information such as marital/relationship status or hobbies for a more personal touch.

Pull out photographs of you with people who have supported you over the years. Do you have any pictures of you with program participants doing the work you love? Post testimonials from satisfied participants or people who can vouch for your work and character.

When your bio is completed, add it to your website, along with an optional picture. People will want to know who you are. Make a webpage entitled, "Who We Are," "Staff" or "Leadership."

Create, or update, your LinkedIn account and include your new position. Ask people to give you recommendations.

Your reputation matters.

# Starting & Building an Awesome Nonprofit Organization for a New Generation

In today's world, everyone is investigating someone. You should do a Google search on your own name and see what comes up. Request websites immediately correct any errors or deficiencies, including asking for removal of slanderous information.

Set up a Google Alert and get a notification email whenever you, and/or your organization, are mentioned in the media. This will also come in handy with all the media coverage you may garner after reading the marketing techniques in Chapter Ten.

## #3    Naming Your Organization

You are giving birth. It's like naming a baby. Make it special and unique. Give it a name which lets the world know what you do. Keep it short and impactful.

Before you begin to use it, check to make sure the domain name is available. A good place to do a search and purchase one is at godaddy.com. It would be a terrible thing if you invested a lot of time in a name, only to learn you cannot use it online.

Also consider abbreviating your nonprofit's if the full name is already taken. For example, Young People Matter (YPM) New York uses ypmnewyork.org.

Only use .ORG for your domain name. It stands for "organization."

We came up with the name of Young People Matter (YPM) through a young person—namely my daughter.

Simone Joye Eford

Legend has it a group of adults were debating in my living room one night. We had spent hours strategizing about how we were going to provide services to young people in Atlanta.
We debated as if we were in a jury room. There were fifteen names that made it to the final round. We were deadlocked.

My daughter, who was 11 years old at the time, kept walking through the area we were in. Always a curious one, I instructed her to go to her room. She surprisingly responded, "Why can't I stay? Don't young people matter? You're talking about kids, right?" It was the cutest thing.

Everyone agreed.

The verdict was in. The name would be: Young People Matter, with the acronym of YPM. Nonprofits love using acronyms by the way.

You will find you may have moments such as this when you build your nonprofit. The lesson I learned was as you think of your own name, ask a potential program participant. You will want it to be attractive to them. Something that will make them come to your door, not just something you feel.

From the naming of the organization, young people were a part of our leadership team. They created our name, designed the logo, and even chose the colors we painted our facility. Our youth board helped design programs and had full-voting member rights on our board of directors. Young people were trained and sat in on employment interviews for potential hires to work in our programs.

From that, they received real life experiences, while helping us ensure the people we hired were able to connect to our participants. Having program participants vested in your organization will take you further faster. Participant attrition was always our strength.

I loved sharing our story to potential funders who could 'feel" the heart of the organization.

**#4:    Create Your Logo**

A logo will brand your nonprofit. It is your identity. Make it appealing. While you create one, you can also think about the colors you will use for your marketing materials.

Today you can get a professional logo created for as little as $5 from freelance artists on places such as Fiverr.com.

**Trademark your logo.** Protect your name from the potential misuse by others. If you personally created (or paid) for the logo, you should trademark it in your own name to protect your rights to the organization but make sure you get board approval. Discuss it with them and get written documentation.

If you have someone else create your logo make sure you have in writing that you (or the corporation) are the owner and not the artist.

To get a trademark you will file an application with the US Trademark Office. The fee starts at $275.

In some cities you can get free legal assistance to help you. The Pro Bono Partnership (probonopartner.org), is an organization of volunteer attorneys who may be willing to prepare your application for free.

## #5:    Apply for Your EIN

Please do not get ripped off. Do not pay anyone to obtain your Employer Identification Number (EIN). It may take you ten minutes to apply yourself online at the IRS website for free. It is so easy, even a teenager can complete it for you.

After you complete your application, your nine-digit number will be immediately generated.

The number is your federal tax id, which is the business equivalent of a social security number. Your EIN will be used so much as you carry on the work of your nonprofit, you will likely memorize it in no time.

There is toss up whether you should list it on your website. You should be aware the nonprofit sector is a full disclosure industry. I can find an organization's EIN number in less than three minutes. Many nonprofits advertise it in the footer of their websites, along with other important designations. Providing it upfront helps prove you are a legitimate charity.

## #6    Apply for Your D-U-N-S Number

Before you can bid on government contracts and apply for federal grant opportunities, you will need to get a DUNS (Data Universal Numbering System) number for your organization. It is free to obtain a DUNS number at dandb.com. Consider your DUNS account as the place for your organization's credit worthiness. You may want to place your DUNS number on your website footer next to your EIN number as well.

## #7     Create Your Mission Statement

You should create your mission statement with extra care. After your nonprofit's name, your mission will be the most used words of your nonprofit.

Think of how you will describe what you do.

What will you say? Now tell it in one or two sentences.

Your mission statement should be short, yet succinct. It should also be posted prominently on your website, social media and in all printed materials.

**Here are examples of great mission statements:**

Kiva: "To connect people through lending to alleviate poverty."

American Heart Association: "Building healthier lives, free of cardiovascular diseases and stroke."

Goodwill Industries International: "Goodwill Industries International enhances the dignity and quality of life of individuals, families and communities by eliminating barriers to opportunity and helping people in need reach their fullest potential through the power of work."

## #8     Create Your Vision Statement

Fairly new to a nonprofit description is a vision statement. This is your statement on how the world is going to view your organization according to the work you do.

Here are some examples of great vision statements compared to a mission statement.

**Mission:** "Seeking to put God's love into action, <u>Habitat for Humanity</u> brings people together to build homes, and hope."

**Vision:** "A world where everyone has a decent place to live."

<u>National Association of Nonprofit Professionals (NANPP)</u>

**Mission**: "To strengthen nonprofit professionals through networking, training, mentoring and professional growth.

**Vision**: "To inspire, motivate and align nonprofit professionals while promoting the value of joining the nonprofit sector."

## #9      Research Potential Funding Sources

After your mission and vision statement, research potential funding opportunities to ensure you have created a viable nonprofit. I call them grant research plans.

It is better to know in the beginning whether you are creating something which can be funded. It really makes little sense to create a nonprofit without seeing whether they are resources out there to assist you.

Creating this list at the start, will save you valuable time. Most new nonprofit leaders search "blindly" for grant opportunities, or invest heavily in program services, only to find out they are limited in their funding prospects.

Chapter Nine highlights funding sources and can be a great place to organize your own prospects.

## #10      File for Incorporation/Articles of Incorporation

All businesses are incorporated with your state's government, likely your Secretary of State.

You file for incorporation using their application. You will need to include a document called the Articles of Incorporation. These are your legal documents for the nonprofit.

Crafting your Articles of Incorporation are easy. Some states require you to identify a president, treasurer and a secretary to incorporate. Others only require one person. You can use your family or friends at this stage on a temporary basis.

Use an office or a post office box for your address. Do not use your personal home address.

Be sure to submit your Articles free of any errors or processing can be delayed. I have seen Articles rejected because we forgot to add the INC at the end of the name. Use the exact name you have listed under your EIN number.

Once the state approves your application, you will receive a Certificate of Incorporation. Make sure to get a certified copy. Your certificate is your official document stating you are a nonprofit corporation in your state.

**#11    Nonprofit    Corporation    vs.    A    Tax-Exempt Nonprofit Corporation**

After you receive the state's approval to operate as a nonprofit corporation, you are not automatically a tax-exempt organization. Only the IRS provides federal tax-exempt status. You will need to get approval from the IRS before you can claim you are an exempt organization.

According to the IRS, to obtain a 501(c)3 tax-exempt "direct service" classification, "An organization must be organized and operated exclusively for exempt purposes *(you exist solely to help others in society)* set forth in section 501(c)(3), and none of its earnings may inure to any private shareholder or individual. *(There are no profits which are distributed to any people like the stock in a for-profit entity)*.

"In addition, it may not be an action organization, *i.e.*, it may not attempt to influence legislation as a substantial part of its activities and it may not participate in any campaign activity for or against political candidates."

This is serious and gets a lot of nonprofits into trouble. You may not lobby for a political candidate. You may not speak against a candidate. If you, or your employees, board members, etc. post anything on social media about politics they should put up a disclaimer stating, "These views are my own." Election? What election? You have no clue.

#### #12    Check for your State's Charity Designation.

Before you collect one dollar from any individual or funding source, be sure to check your state's charitable giving guidelines. Thirty-seven states and the District of Columbia require charitable solicitation registration and renewals. This is an important, and often overlooked, requirement which can cost you hundreds or thousands of dollars in non-compliance fees.

Registration is usually about $20 or $30 dollars and assists the state government in reducing fraudulent fundraising practices and scams.

**State Exemptions.** With a 501(c)3 tax exemption you may not have to pay corporate taxes. Unfortunately, in some states you will still have to pay other taxes, such as sales and property taxes. Check to see if you qualify for any exemptions in your state. If you do, just imagine how much you will save by making tax-free purchases. Also, in some jurisdictions, use those "tax-free back to school" sales to purchase your office supplies in places like Walmart.

**#13    Open your Bank Account.** Be sure to check to see which bank offers the most to a small business. Services like free checking, free or low monthly fees, etc.

To open your bank account, you will need your Certificate of Incorporation and a physical address.

It is recommended you have two signatories on your account (you as the founder/executive director and, your treasurer or board president).

To reduce the risk of fraudulent activity, members of your fiscal staff, (or financial consultants) should not be signatories, or have access to withdrawals, on your account.

You can decide whether you want to provide other staff members with debit cards for purchases.

Do not use your home address for your bank account and use a different banking institution than the one you use for your personal banking. Try your best to keep your personal funds separate from your nonprofit accounts.

Save on the costs of purchasing checks from the bank. Use your starter checks until you find you need additional ones. Vistaprint.com is a great place to order checks, as well as your business cards and marketing materials at reasonable costs.

If you can, open a free savings account and set aside funds to create your organization's reserve (savings) fund.

## #14    Location/Space.

Where are you going to operate? It is time to think of a physical location for your administrative office and services. This is where you will put your networking skills to work.

In the nonprofit world, if you do not have space to operate—a place where your program participants visit, you are not yet in business.

There are some who share space with other nonprofits. Others use libraries and schools to conduct program "events." That is not running a nonprofit.

At the end of the day, you will need your own space, with your own desk and chair to operate.

Are you planning on operating out of your home? Forget it! That is not a viable option for many reasons. Can you recall ever going to someone's home for social services? It will be almost impossible to get insurance coverage if you operate your nonprofit out of your home.

Consider an online search for "nonprofit incubators" which are low-costs spaces you can share with other nonprofits. Check on Craigslist for spaces available for lease. Google "space for nonprofits" in your town. Contact people at larger nonprofits, as well as schools, and ask if they have space.

In lieu of paying market rent, you can offer to pay for additional security or maintenance services? Maybe you can help with getting volunteer support if repairs are needed. You can also contact a realtor and ask if they have any clients who may have unused space, such as an empty house, which has been hard to sell or rent.

If anyone allows you the use of space, whether renting or free, get all the terms in writing either through a lease agreement or a written Memorandum of Agreement (MOA).

You should also seek out elected officials who may be aware of unused or underutilized government property. The federal government has surplus property across the nation. Google federal government surplus property. Search and see if your state government has surplus property as well.

Whatever space you decide upon, before you sign on the dotted line and hire the moving truck, thoroughly check for any local zoning requirements and any information you may need to get a Certificate of Occupancy.

This area can be a major hassle. There may be zoning restrictions on what can operate in a certain location. You may need to obtain an architect to provide you with building plans. You may need to pay for an inspection. You may need two exits instead of one. There are many questions you will need answered.

You are opening a public entity and there are many rules and regulations to protect the safety of the public. Make sure you check thoroughly and diligently. Failure to do so can set you back months from a grand opening. You also risk being shut down by government officials, or worse someone can get hurt at your site.

**#15     We Have the Space, Now What?**

Do not sit in it alone. Create a position available for interns and send to colleges in your area if you cannot yet hire staff. In exchange for the experience and college credits you are building your team.

Recruit volunteers and give them, along with interns, "work shifts." The hours should coincide with the hours you are open to your program participants.

Put together a donor email request and send to every furniture place you know for donations. Banks are also great places to find used furniture in excellent condition.

Add your nonprofit's new address to Google online so people can find you in Google maps.

Start providing services.

Every employer must comply with the requirements of the Occupational Safety and Health Act (OSHA) and provide a workplace primarily free of hazards. To learn about the rules and regulations, visit osha.gov.

Remember to display workplace posters. You can get them for free, or a reduced rate from OSHA and your state's labor department.

## CHAPTER 5
# Making It Legit: Governance

*"Management is doing things right;*
*leadership is doing the right things."*
*Peter Drucker*

Starting a nonprofit is not a solo venture. The nonprofit is not a private business. Nor does any individual(s) "own" it. Founders can become easily attached which is against tax-exemption regulations.

Nonprofits are a tax-free business, governed by a Board of Directors or a Board of Trustees. In exchange for charitable work and fiscal transparency, it does not have to pay taxes. This inspires confidence in potential donors and funders. Your status demonstrates your organization has a legitimate charitable purpose, a structure for accomplishing its goals, and is accountable to the public.

You will need to think who will serve in your leadership roles. Make sure their reputations and public persona are reputation ready. As you seek leadership, ask them if there is anything in their background which could be deemed as embarrassing for your charity.

You do not want anyone governing the organization if they have ever been guilty of fraudulent financial activities. Trust me, funders will find out and keep it to themselves as they send you one funding rejection letter after another.

For incorporation purposes you may have already identified your president, treasurer and secretary.

Now you can continue to recruit other members of your "founding board." At the bare minimum you will need a president, treasurer and secretary. Add in a chairperson and these people will be members of your board's "executive committee."

Be sure to hold a board vote for each person you recruit if you do not yet have a board nominating committee.

There is no set number of board members required by law, but you should keep the number at an odd number in case you need a tie-breaker for voting purposes.

## By-Laws: Your Nonprofit's Constitution

Your By-Laws are very important nonprofit documents.

Consider them your constitution, like the one we have for the United States of America. Board members provide governance over the organization through the By-Laws and via voting privileges.

The By-Laws outline how the board functions, meeting schedule, duties of members and other laws to guide the nonprofit. You should also include information stating what happens to the organization's assets should the organization dissolve.

They should be crafted with care as they should be used to govern your nonprofit for many years to come. Any changes to the By-Laws in the future must be made through a board vote.

I am always in awe at the lackadaisical attitude some nonprofit leaders possess regarding their By-Laws.

One founder once relayed, "We don't follow them. I haven't dusted those things off since we wrote them years ago."

They were irrelevant until a funder read a copy and found out her board had not been meeting as outlined. Consequently, that organization blew a funding opportunity.

Your By-Laws will also be included with your tax-exempt application to the IRS. My colleagues and I often joke the IRS will review them under a microscope.

After your By-Laws are completed make them an agenda item for your first "official" board meeting. Be sure to get each member to approve, sign and date the final versions which should all be originals. You keep one of the originals, along with your board secretary.

You can find samples of By-Laws at grantspace.org.

## *Protecting Yourself: Potential Removal of Founder*

There are some who will debate me on what you are getting to read, but just know Simone is on hashtag #TeamFounder.

Having stated that, let me share with a rare exception no one should ever be allowed to remove the nonprofit's founder as the head of the nonprofit. The only exception would be if you committed a criminal, or other shameful, act. In that case you would likely go to prison or resign anyway.

Other than that, there should only be two reasons a founder leaves a nonprofit, through resignation or through death. Of course, your organization may outgrow your leadership and it may come a time for you to move on, but it should be done at your convenience. Voting for a founder's removal should not even be an option.

You are the creator. It's your vision. Your idea. Your passion. Your sweat. Your sacrifice. You are the person who built the organization from scratch. You've bought the books, done the research and the work. You recruited the board.

When you research what By-Laws consists of you will likely not find a section on the founder's role. Add your own. There is no law, or regulation, that states you cannot.

The section should describe your terms of service and a description of your duties. You should also state there is no other staff (paid or unpaid) position higher than the founder/executive director.

Set the leadership tone early.

Once the money starts coming in, people change. There may be some who are envious of your success. You know the same people you invited to become a part of the history you are making. The people who are volunteers. People who lend you their name and encouragement. Then one day you will wake up and they will have decided you are no longer needed. Can you imagine?

Trust me on this one. Protect yourself from the word go. Religious and other nonprofit leaders are filled with horror stories of their attempted takeovers. Do not let it happen to you.

## *Terms of Board Service*

Your board members should carefully consider the terms of service and have the entire body vote on it. Two years, with renewable terms are about the average. Some members have served on boards for decades through re-election, or worse, self-appointment.

The founder/executive director should be an ex officio member of the board, meaning you should not have voting privileges. Your term on the board should be perpetual.

## *Conflict of Interest Policy Statement*

Every board member needs to sign off on a conflict of interest statement.

The IRS states, "A conflict of interest occurs where individuals' obligation to further the organization's charitable purpose is at odds with their own financial interests."

In other words, do not lease space from a building affiliated with a board member (or yourself) and then pay the rent from the nonprofit's funds.

Another area of conflict is when board members receive a salary for their service. Board members should never be paid. You can reimburse them for expenses that benefit the organization (transportation to meetings, office supplies, etc.).

A conflict of interest signed statement should also be included with your IRS application for tax-exemption and should be signed by each member.

Whenever a new board member joins your organization, mare sure they should sign this statement.

### *Applying for Your 501(C)3 IRS Tax Exemption*

The IRS report there are more 60,000 applications pending for new nonprofits. They also state the process can take up to nine months for processing. The absolute worse time to file for a new nonprofit is during the annual tax season (January – April) when IRS agents are busy with income tax returns.

The longest I ever had to wait for any exemption was ninety days and that seems long to me.

After years of experience I have learned the IRS is not seeking to determine whether you should exist as a tax-exempt organization. They are searching for the reason you should not have a tax-exemption. The burden of proof relies on you being able to show you are going to be a legitimate charity.

If you complete the longer 1023, or are requested to send in additional information, be clear about your purpose. Keep in mind the reason why your organization should not pay taxes. Integrity is a must. Let them know your passion. Share activities which tell what you have already done, rather than a document full of what "we plan to do."

# Starting & Building an Awesome Nonprofit Organization for a New Generation

Many individuals hope to receive a tax-exemption to avoid paying business taxes for a for-profit business or to launder money. The IRS seeks to avoid granting such fraudulent entities tax-exemptions, and they do it well.

*Completing Your Application for Recognition of Tax-Exempt Status.*

To begin, you can find all the information to help you complete your 1023 at the IRS website.

Churches, synagogues, temples, and mosques are automatically considered tax-exempt and are not required to file a 1023.

Others who are automatically exempt are "integrated auxiliaries of churches and conventions or association of churches and any organization that has gross receipts in each taxable year of normally not more than $5,000."

There are three filing fees depending upon the gross receipts of your organization.

**Form 1023 EZ** - $275 – This one is as easy as filling out a postcard. You can file a 1023EZ if you are not a church, a school, a hospital, a foreign organization, or a medical research organization and your total projected revenue (gross receipts) is less than $50,000 per year. You also may not have assets more than $250,000. Before you file complete the Form 1023-EZ Eligibility Worksheet on the IRS website. The IRS states most organizations, including 70 percent of all applicants, qualify for Form 1023 EZ and

Form 1023, includes 26 pages of questions. You will also have to include a statement of activities and a detailed budget.

You file Form 1023 if your organization's gross receipts do not exceed $10,000 or less annually over a 4-year period. The application fee is $400.

If your gross receipts exceed $10,000 annually over a 4-year period, your application fee is $850.

If you hire someone to complete your Form 1023 (long form), I would not pay anyone more than $800 for its completion.

***Fiscal Year***

Your fiscal year is the period you will use for accounting purposes and preparation of your financial statements. Many nonprofits use July 1 – June 30th to coincide with the government's fiscal year and public grant cycles. Others may operate on a calendar year (January 1 – December 31). You and your treasurer should determine which is best for your

## We Are Tax-Exempt. Now What?

After you are approved, the IRS will send you a "Determination Letter." The letter will be your proof of your tax-exempt status. Make a PDF and keep electronically. You will need this letter for donors.

Notify your Board of Directors and put that tax-exemption to work. It's time to solicit product donations from your local businesses and corporations.

# Starting & Building an Awesome Nonprofit Organization for a New Generation

For the first few years, we received donations from United Way and Staples. In fact, Staples donations allowed us to set up our entire administrative office with a computer, printer, pens, paper, etc. I will forever be thankful.

Do not overlook cultivation of potential prospects. In other words, find people who you can beg for donations. You will be doing a lot of it to get the things you need.

After every donation, send a thank you letter, place their logo on your website, give them credit and if you want, attach a link to their website.

Once your tax-exemption is approved it will be listed in a central database called the IRS Exempt Organization Master File/IRS Select Check and in the database of GuideStar.org. The IRS file and GuideStar are the leading sources for donors to check to see if you are a legitimate charity.

The IRS database is updated quarterly. Be sure to check your status. After you receive your Determination Letter, if you find your nonprofit has not been listed, give the IRS a call to learn of the next update. If you are not listed, your chances for donations and grants are reduced by the donors who will check there before contributing.

GuideStar states it is, "The world's largest source of information on nonprofit organizations." The public can review your 990s and read reviews on your organization. It is wise for you to register on their site, and update the account which was already generated for your nonprofit after your IRS approval.

GuideStar issues transparency seals (bronze, silver and gold) based upon how much information a charity has voluntarily shared on their website as a gauge to determine a charity worthiness. Nonprofits then add it to their website donor pages.

CharityNavigator.org is another source for legitimate tax-exempt nonprofit listings.

Also, if you ever change your address, you can request the IRS update and provide you with an Affirmation Letter.

## *Collecting Online Donations*

Set up your website to accept donations through a third-party source such as PayPal who provides nonprofit discounts.

Take advantage of PayPal's mobile card reader and "PayPal Here" app so you can collect donations from anywhere on your smart phone or tablet. You never know when someone will want to donate to you while you are out and about.

It happened to me in the strangest of all places—a car dealership.

As I sat waiting for my car to be serviced, I struck up a conversation with a man who inquired what I did for a living.

When I told him about the organization, he wanted to donate $300 on the spot. With the card reader, I was able to swipe his card on my iPad, email him a receipt, save his details to send a thank you note and add him to our donor database.

PayPal to the rescue.

You can also check out Donorbox.org which is free if you get less than $1k in donations per month. Above $1K, they charge a fee of .89% for the month's donation. Also, if you use WordPress for your website, check out their donation plugin called Give.

### Nonprofit Postage Rates

Did you know certain nonprofits qualify for postal discounts? Go to the United States Post Office site (usps.com) to see you if you qualify and to enroll.

# CHAPTER 6
# Setting Up Operations

*"Don't ever let your business get ahead of the financial side of your business. Accounting, accounting, accounting. Know your numbers." Tilman J. Fertitta*

## Managing the Money: Accounting Controls

There are many benefits to having an organization with tax-exempt status. There are also major responsibilities. One of them is keeping excellent financial records backed up by a paper trail.

In addition, make sure you and your treasurer, keep up with any tax changes. There is a lot going on right now in the nonprofit sector regarding tax laws.

### *Accounting Principles*

First and foremost, hire a bookkeeper, even if it's on a part-time basis if you cannot afford someone full-time. Consider them working remotely. Technology has allowed anyone to be able to log into your financial software from the convenience of their home or office.

Refrain from attempting to manage your own accounting. One set of eyes on the financials is never the best option in the nonprofit world. You also do not want to give the appearance you are running a solo enterprise.

### Cash vs. Accrual Accounting Methods

Nonprofits must adhere to GAAP (generally accepted accounting principles). You can read more about GAAP (pronounced "gap"). at accounting.com.

In the start-up phase you can use the cash method which is easier according to accountants. Smaller nonprofits without any paid staff or government funding can get away with it on a temporary basis.

As you grow, and obtain more funding, especially any government funding you will need to use the accrual method.

### Choosing Financial Software

There is a plethora of financial software available for nonprofits.

QuickBooks is the leading the way and make it very easy for nonprofits. Check out QuickBooks for Nonprofits and take a test run. Your first 30 days are free.

Whatever software you decide, make sure it is compatible with the development (fundraising) side of the nonprofit. QuickBooks has a handy feature which allows you to connect a donor database to your financials.

### *The 990 Tax Documents*

On May 31$^{st}$ of each year, the IRS will be awaiting your nonprofit's yearly tax returns known as the IRS Form 990 *Return of Organization Exempt from Income Tax.*

Your returns will consist of twelve months of financial information, including all those receipts you have been meticulously keeping.

A 990 is a nonprofit's most important tax document. The 990 allows the IRS, donors and the public, to see the financial health and operations of a nonprofit.

It is filled with information which will shine a spotlight on the fiscal accountability of your nonprofit.

Timely returns are your goal. If you think your return will be late, you can make a written extension request via IRS Form 8868. You will then have five more months to make the extension deadline of October 31$^{st}$. Late penalties are between $20 up to $10,000 *per day.*

If you fail to file your 990 for three consecutive years, your tax exemption will be revoked.

Even if your nonprofit's gross revenue is $0, you should still file to show you are in operation and create a public financial record.

No public record? People will believe you are not operating, or a poor business to invest their dollars.

That is not the image you want to ever portray. If you are not ready to prepare the financial accountability of your nonprofit, you should not ask for donations. There are many other nonprofits who could use that funding.

### *How to File Your 990*

There are three forms which are used to file your annual tax returns. You file them according to your nonprofit's income. If your:

Gross receipts are less than $50,000 – Use the IRS 990N E-Postcard.

Gross receipts are under $200,000 and total assets under $500,000 - Use the IRS 990EZ (short form).

Gross receipts total $200,000+ or your assets total $500,000 – Use the IRS 990 (long form).

Many nonprofits use accountants, or financial consultants, to complete their 990s. If you decide to complete it yourself, you can download the forms directly from the IRS website. Express990.com and file990.org also provide do-it-yourself forms you can complete online.

The entire board should review the 990s before filing and the executive director is person who usually signs them.

You will always need to demonstrate your fiscal responsibility. Every year. By filing your 990 proves to your donors, and of course the IRS, your nonprofit is committed to fiscal transparency.

Your 990s can also be posted on your website which is always a plus for the public and potential donors. Also, remember you can view the 990s of any nonprofit in America with your GuideStar account.

### Create A Fiscal Policy Manual

Work with your treasurer and create a manual which will keep everyone on the same accord regarding financial matters of the organization. Create your system for checks and balances.

Here are a few tips I highlight for my clients:

- Never make a payment to any vendor, or an individual, without a detailed invoice.
- Never accept a cash donation. If you do, the cash should be deposited in the bank within 24 hours.

The person who collects a check on the behalf of the organization should not be the person to deposit the check.

Each check should be logged in a binder. A paper copy is not necessary, but the check number, bank, name of the donor should be kept each month.

At the end of each month, when your fiscal person reconciles your bank statements, make sure you check the logs.

### The B Word: Your Nonprofit Budget

Your budget is your fiscal blueprint. It is a word you use often.

When you're asked, "What's your budget?" Make sure you have an accurate answer. There is nothing worse than a nonprofit leader who has no idea what their budget is. That's a serious red flag.

# Starting & Building an Awesome Nonprofit Organization for a New Generation

Everything about a nonprofit is governed by "the budget." Your entire existence will be determined by it. You should conduct your nonprofit's work based upon your financial resources.

Your treasurer will stay busy reviewing budgets. Every funding request will require one so make sure they are consistent.

There are various types of budgets. There are budgets for programs and an organizational budget for all operations.

You should create your first year's budget prior to operating. For your strategic plan, a long-term budget of three years is best.

Each year, pick a month to estimate the next year's operating budget. Board review and approval is a must before you execute your budget.

The following are basic budget items traditionally found in a nonprofit operational budget.

### INCOME
Government
Foundations
Corporations
Individuals
Fundraisers/Special Events
In-Kind Donations
Fee for Services
Interest Income
Endowment

**EXPENSES**

Personnel Services (unless your organization is an all-volunteer led organization, your personnel will likely always be your largest expense).

-includes all staff and their hourly salary x hours per week=yearly salary

-fringe benefits (includes taxes, unemployment insurance, social security and Medicare deductions; also includes optional deductions for health insurance, vision the organization pays on behalf of its employees, etc.)

OTPS (Other Than Personnel Services)

-all other expenses (occupancy, supplies, equipment, utilities, marketing, transportation, printing, miscellaneous, travel, professional development, indirect costs, etc.)

You can find some great budget samples at
https://www.template.net/business/budget-templates/nonprofit-budget-template/

***Nonprofit Insurance***

At the beginning of starting a nonprofit my largest frustration was my first attempt at purchasing nonprofit insurance. I thought I could just pick up the phone and get a policy as easy as I could for a home or my car. Wrong.

To save you a lot of time, contact the Nonprofit Insurance Alliance Group (insurancefornonprofits.org). Based in Santa Cruz, CA they provide insurance coverage for nonprofits in thirty-two states. You cannot purchase directly through them. Most nonprofit insurance can only be obtained exclusively through insurance brokers and agents. However, their website details helpful information on the nonprofit insurance industry and has a lot of risk management information.

### *Types of Insurance Coverage*

### General Liability

Covers damages if a non-employee is injured on the organization's property, such as a slip and fall. (Employees are covered under workers' compensation insurance). General liability insurance is also called commercial general liability insurance.

**Director's & Officers Liability** insurance, also known as D&O policy.

Covers board members and directors against personally being named in a lawsuit should someone want to sue the organization.

Without it, you and your board can be sued for your personal assets. Could you imagine losing your personal home in a lawsuit? Get this policy as quickly as possible.

A D&O policy usually does not cover criminal or fraudulent behavior. Make sure your policy covers employment-related claims (e.g., harassment, discrimination, etc.) which seem to be the most claims filed against nonprofit leadership.

**Property** insurance covers furniture, supplies, computers, etc. in your office.

**Professional Liability** insurance, aka malpractice insurance covers the organization against workplace claims such as discrimination or sexual harassment.

**Product Liability** insurance should be purchased if you plan on selling products to the public including something as small as baked cookies.

**Insurance Riders.** Ask an insurance professional about additional riders you may need according to the program participants you serve. For example, if you are a child-serving agency you will may be required by law to obtain coverage for the protection of children.

**Health Insurance.** Do you have personal health care coverage? What will you do if you get sick? Begin researching plans if needed for yourself and determine how you will need if you plan to offer them to your employees.

Under the health reform's employer mandate requirement, if you have under 50 full-time employees you are not required to offer health benefits to employees. When you grow and choose to offer these benefits follow other nonprofits who are offering individual health insurance and reimbursing employees' premiums, or a portion of premiums, as well as qualified medical expenses through a Small Business Health Reimbursement Arrangement (HRA). You can read about this option at Zanebenefits.com.

You can also visit the National Council of Nonprofits' website councilofnonprofits.org. In the search bar, type "Frequently Asked Questions by Nonprofits About the Affordable Care Act." You will find a slew of information.

## *Human Resources*

The first thing you should decide is what type of attendance system you are going to use to report work time. Will you use handwritten timesheets? Or will you use an electronic time clock?

Your fiscal staff may want to save the trees and have an electronic system. Government funding sources and auditors will prefer paper copies. You can make a combination of both.

Whichever you decide you should have documentation for everyone's time, in and out of your office, including volunteers. **Create Your Organizational Chart** Even if you cannot hire every position at this time, it is important you know what a good nonprofit team consists of.

### *Nonprofit Titles: A Different Language*

We speak a different language in the nonprofit sector beginning with what we call ourselves at work.

Large national organizations, such as the Covenant House tend to follow more corporate titles as noted earlier (CEO vs. Executive Director). Hospitals tend to have a Board of Trustees rather than a Board of Directors.

### *Here are the titles and positions used by nonprofits.*

**Board Leadership** – Chairperson, President, Secretary and Treasurer. The rest of the board are called members or trustees.

**Administrative/Operations**

Executive director ("aka the E.D."), CEO (usual the title in a large national nonprofit); Founder

Deputy Director (VP) (Usually over operations which includes fiscal, HR, IT, facility/maintenance)

Associate Executive Director (Second VP; usually over programming)

Fiscal (Director) (Manager) (Coordinator)

-Bookkeeper; Accounts Payable; Accounts Receivable; Payroll

Development (VP) (Chief Development Officer) (Director) (Manager) or (Coordinator)

-Grant Writer; Grants Manager; Planned Giving; Special Events, Research, Development Assistant. Usually over marketing area.

Public Relations/Marketing (Director) (Manager) or (Coordinator)

Human Resources (Director) (Manager) or (Coordinator)

   -Payroll Manager (Clerk)

IT (Director; Manager; Coordinator)

Executive Assistant (the assistant usually works for the Executive Director)

## Program

Program Director (Manager) (Coordinator)

Program Assistant

Volunteers and Interns

## Volunteers

Volunteers are at the heart of every nonprofit. You will not survive without them.

Every volunteer, even those assisting with one-day events, should complete a volunteer application where you collect their home address, telephone and a reason why they want to work with your nonprofit.

As part of the volunteer (and employment) screening process, you should also research where you can get background checks done and be sure every volunteer undergoes a background check. Background checks from your local police department may be cheaper than your state's child welfare agency (which may also offer this service).

On your website make sure you have a volunteer sign-up button in a prominent place and a page dedicated to volunteers. The leading source for volunteer recruitment is volunteermatch.org.

America's premiere volunteer corps is AmeriCorps and Senior Corps (nationalservice.org). Even as a start-up you should review their application and apply when you qualify. It is an awesome program in which the federal government pays the salaries for a nonprofit employee. Think of it as the domestic Peace Corps-- volunteers at home.

Check out the Taproot Foundation (taproot.org) which connects, "Nonprofits and social change organizations with passionate, skilled volunteers who share their expertise pro bono."

Taproot links you with professional volunteers in marketing, strategy, HR, and IT. I have used them in the past and have met some great people willing to lend a hand for short-term projects.

### *Personnel Manual/Employee Handbook*

Although you may not have any staff yet, you should begin to draft your employee policies ensuring they adhere to federal, state and local guidelines for employment.

This is also the time you begin to set up a system for your personnel files. For each employee you hire, you will need a separate file for them. Keep their medical and I-9 forms, which document an employee's immigration status, in a separate file. All personnel records should always be stored in a locked file cabinet.

### *Hiring Staff*

There is no magic time to hire staff in a start-up. Obviously, you will hire staff when you are financially able to do so. The first line of your hiring pool should go to your dedicated volunteers, including founding board members if they qualify for the position(s) you need.

Your priority for hires should be a person to help with your fiscal responsibilities and your fundraising (development department). Remember where you read earlier what a great team looks like? Here are a few reasons why you should ensure a good balance between operations and programming.

Funders may not believe you can manage their money if you do not have the correct leadership in place.

If everyone is running the programs, who is managing the money and resources for legal compliance, growth and sustainability?

Also, it is important to note founders/executive directors may burn out quickly managing all aspects of the nonprofit. Those are the times you will want to quit. You must find your balance to ensure this does not happen.

### *Advertising for Nonprofit Employees*

Make detailed job descriptions for the team you are expecting. You want to ensure experienced nonprofit candidates will apply for your positions, so try and advertise within the nonprofit community first before going to general employment sites like Indeed.com.

Many will allow you to post on their job boards for free, or a very low cost. Some of the great ones are nanpp.org, idealist.org, nonprofitjobs.org, execsearches.com, and opportunitynocs.org.

### *Payroll and Taxes*

Nonprofit employers handle payroll and taxes very similar to a for-profit business.

Nonprofits must withhold Social Security, federal and state taxes, as well as Medicare. Nonprofits also pay federal and state unemployment taxes.

This information is reported on your IRS 941 the *Employer's Quarterly Tax Return.*

Nonprofits follow workers' compensation laws which is another fee you should be ready to pay when you begin a payroll.

Setting up this area is complex and should be done with diligent care. Your government reporting must always be error free or it can spiral into many late nights.

A payroll service (or experienced fiscal employee) will likely handle this area from start to finish.

I am going to give a shameless plug for the company ADP to handle your payroll and reporting. They seem to work with nonprofits more easily than other companies I have used. They can be convinced to provide your nonprofit with a discount simply by asking. Second, they get this right and if they make an error, they immediately investigate it quickly and correct it.

Fees for their services vary and depends upon the number of employees. The higher the number of employers the higher your monthly fee. The most I've ever paid with a payroll of 15 people was about $135 per month which included all state and federal reporting, our bi-weekly payroll, and generation of year-end W2s and 1099s for employees and consultants.

There are many other service providers including independent payroll agents. You can also inquire with your bank as some larger ones now offer payroll services.

When you hire your first employee contact your state's labor department. If you forget, no worries, they will likely contact you first once your nonprofit's certificate of incorporation is generated.

When you receive your state ID number, make sure you keep it in a safe place. You will need it when you hire staff along with your state's unemployment insurance and workers' compensation accounts. You will also need to use the number when you apply for state grants.

# Starting & Building an Awesome Nonprofit Organization for a New Generation

## *Risk Management*

Nonprofits live close to the edge of disaster. Whether you fail to make a payroll, or you find out someone working with children on your staff is a pedophile, the risks are there.

As a small nonprofit, you may feel you have little risk. That may not be the case. The best time to prepare for a storm are when the waters are calm.

***Disaster Plan.*** Make your plan if a natural disaster strikes. If there is an emergency, where is your safe location? Who is the point of contact? Where will program participants find you in the case of a disaster? Visit Ready.gov and put together your plan.

***People Are Shady.*** Whenever I speak to a group of nonprofit leaders I share there are people who make a living attempting to sue nonprofits. Many nonprofit leaders are jaded because of it. Many have been taken advantage of by people they trusted.

Nonprofits are a business which carries a large amount of insurance and that is alluring to criminals.

Over the years, I have worked with executive directors, board members, and attorneys who had to deal with visitors who allegedly had accidental falls, burned their hands from the bathroom's hot water, got food poisoning, and even a volunteer who used the organization's information to create a fake bank account. The stories are endless, and any organization can be victimized.

I can recall a time an employee claimed she had breast cancer. The entire agency rallied behind her and were sympathetic. They put together an emergency fund for her.

Then she threatened to sue citing her illness was due to a workplace condition.

She was not telling the truth. That is how low some people will go for a quick payoff.

She failed to think ahead and had no idea employees are covered by workers' compensation. When she was told she would need to file a claim with a government entity, she left that day and never returned.

How will you handle such matters? If you think you can trust anyone, that's fine, but be prepared.

Think ahead.

Financial insolvency is also a huge risk as well. At the website, oliverwyman.com you can read the 20-page report called, "*Risk Management for Nonprofits*" which highlights the 2015 bankruptcy of FEGS. Once upon a time they were New York City's largest social service nonprofit and crumbled due to financial mismanagement and owing creditors millions.

---

## CHAPTER 7
# Founder vs. the Executive Director

---

*"At first they will ask why you're doing it.*
*Later they'll ask how you did it."*

When Eric Schmidt, the Executive Chairman of Google was asked to tell his favorite business line, he answered, "Get a coach."

Today, I want you to consider me as your personal coach.

I wrote this chapter to highlight your role as the gifted, phenomenal and selfless person who will carry the title of founder *and* executive director.

A founder and executive director are two distinct positions. There are nonprofit executive directors who were never founders but not vice versa.

As a founder your issues are vastly different from a person who entered a nonprofit already up and running. The resources, the board, the connections, the program participants and the funding were already in place.

As a founder you are putting all those things together.

Another huge difference is where a hired executive director comes from vs. a founder.

### *Who Are Executive Directors?*

Many hired executive directors come from the corporate sector with business connections board members hope will be used as leverage to financially support the organization. I call them "Corporate 101s" who may want to make a career change or come to the nonprofit sector because they want to "give back."

Noble indeed.

Because most board members are corporate executives themselves, it makes sense they are more inclined to recruit and hire those they already know.

Next on the list are leaders who may have served as a board member for the nonprofit. They may be hired as the executive director (or interim executive director) to serve as convenient placeholder until an external candidate can be vetted. In the position, they are usually overwhelmed and create disasters the next executive director must come in and clean up.

Then there are executive directors with a heavy social work/human services background. They are used to the "front lines" from a clinical and theoretical viewpoint. They are needed in social services, but may lack the critical operational skill set for the management of the nonprofit, including the supervision of staff.

The absolute best executive director, in my opinion, is the fundraising expert who possess an entrepreneur mindset.

Fundraisers, (aka the Development Director) obtain a well-rounded view of all areas of a nonprofit. They are involved with every area (programming, client services, fiscal, HR, marketing, promotion and the board).

Many boards have yet to admit, first and foremost, an executive director is a fundraiser, marketing expert and social entrepreneur.

When boards lack this critical thought, I am willing to bet they do not have executive directors who stay long and/or keep them out of financial trouble.

I also believe an ideal executive director is one who came up the nonprofit ladder. They may have started out as a volunteer, a client, or even like I did, a grant writer. They have a well-rounded view of not only running a business, a passion for the mission, but also know the nonprofit sector.

This is not to say you do not need an executive director who has a strong background in programming. However, programming is the easiest part of a nonprofit. It's quickly scalable and there are so many who need help you will likely not have to work hard at getting participants for your services.

Nonprofit founders are different.

They hail from various career backgrounds. Some may have been former program participants, volunteers or felt strongly about a community need. Others may be frustrated nonprofit employees.

Their education level varies. They may not have a college degree wherein most hired executive director have completed the bachelor's level.

Founders usually have one thing in common, regardless of their education or career background, and that is a fierce passion. It is that drive that launches a nonprofit.

However, because they are likely new to the sector, as their corporate counterparts, they have much more to learn and digest.

### Who is the Founder?

Founders are like celebrities. You are a public figure and everything you do at your nonprofit is public information. From your salary to the amount of money you raise.

You will also make friends, lots of friends. You will be in a position of prestige for your work. People will praise you because you started a business. One night you may attend a black-tie affair to pick up an award for your work and then you will return to your office to find you have to take out the trash.

It keeps you humble.

Stay approachable even to your haters—you will have those as well.

Remember you are a leader. Many people will look up to you because you are helping to change lives. Some may depend on you to feed their family.

Program participants and their families will want to speak with you. People will depend on your humanity. You should always work like the leader you would want to work for. The spirit of "my door is always open" will work wonders.

You will always need a public spokesperson. You will need more of a public presence because you started from scratch.

# Starting & Building an Awesome Nonprofit Organization for a New Generation

You will likely be stressed out and will need to think of ways to manage it.

You may think you will be working to help people on the front lines of the organization, but most of your time will be spent working with administrative and operational matters.

If you are an introvert, you will need to hire an internal staff person (usually the deputy director or your development director) to serve as "the face" and "the voice" of the organization and your cause. Your board president can also serve in that capacity if they have the time.

You should also seek out training and professional development opportunities geared towards nonprofit founders. You will need to network, learn to cultivate donors and gain access to their circle. You will need to do this while simultaneously running operations and supervising programming.

You will need to hire a coach to help motivate you and to set you up for success. If you attempt to do this alone, you will likely burn out before the end of your second year.

## *Paying Yourself: The Founder's Salary*

As a founder, do not let your board decide your initial salary. You should submit a figure to them. Most board members are not equipped to properly decide compensation of a hired executive director, let alone a founder. They usually base it upon their own work experience, which is likely in the corporate sector.

You should determine your own salary based upon your organizational budget and the number of employees. This way you can be sure you are following the U.S. federal law which states that nonprofits should pay "reasonable compensation."

### *How to Determine Your Salary.*

When you determine your salary, just keep in mind excessive compensation may be perceived as a conflict of interest. When I determine salaries, it is based upon the organization's budget. For example, if your yearly organizational budget is $200,000. Requesting a salary of $50,000 per year, plus another 10% or so for your fringe benefits, is not excessive.

To determine equitable salaries, see what other executive directors (or other staff positions) in your town are earning.

You can look up current job openings which may list the salaries of counterparts. You can also do a Google search using the words, "the salary of (name of ED at X organization).

Another way is to review their IRS 990s on GuideStar.org or CharityNavigator.org. In the 990, look under the section Part VII Compensation of Officers, Directors, Trustees, Key Employees, Highest Compensated Employees, and Independent Contractors. Any nonprofit employee's salary or consultant who earns over $100,000 must be disclosed (but there are rarely repercussions if they do not disclose it).

When you are not earning anything, write down how much you want to earn and print it. Then get a frame and hang it over your desk. Put it out into the universe. When the going gets tough, look at it and remember your goal.

# Starting & Building an Awesome Nonprofit Organization
# for a New Generation

The salary you may want may not happen in year one, or even year two, but it will likely come if you do not give up. Hopefully the information found in this book series will help you.

My first "decent" paycheck, meaning one I could live on without touching my savings, for the nonprofit I founded took four years. Those years sped by.

It was from a $600,000 federal grant which launched the first homeless youth shelter in DeKalb County, GA.

My board felt I deserved twenty percent for my salary. I had written a lower salary in the grant and I wanted to provide job opportunities to others. I took a lower salary and just made sure I had adequate health coverage.

Had I accepted the board suggested amount, I would have not been able to properly invest in our infrastructure and hire the paid staff I had longed for.

It worked out well and I would do it again. Greed has no place when you are building a nonprofit. I knew I would earn more sooner or later.

Also, your salary may be earmarked across multiple funding streams. Nonprofit salaries can come from various pots. Ten percent may come from Foundation A. Another forty percent from Corporation X and the remaining fifty percent from a government grant and unrestricted funds. This is another reason why you must have excellent financial controls. You do not want to misuse funding.

Consider there are some executive directors in all volunteer-led organizations, like standupforkids.org, who do not earn a salary at all. In lieu of one, they may receive housing assistance, a company vehicle and financial stipends.

You will need to think about the model that fits you best.

## Where to Obtain Your Salary

If you have not yet secured enough funding to pay yourself, the following foundations give thousands of dollars for start-up capital, executive director salaries and technical assistance to launch organizations and build capacity. You can search for others online.

At Echoing Green, you can read about some exciting start-ups and social entrepreneurs from around the world.

| Echoing Green Foundation 462 Seventh Ave – 13th Floor New York, NY 10018 212-689-1165 echoinggreen.org | Draper Richards Kaplan Foundation 1600 El Camino Real, Suite 155 Menlo Park, CA 94025 650-319-7808 draperrichards.org | John D. and Catherine T. MacArthur Foundation 161 N. Clark St., Suite 700 Chicago, IL 60601 (312) 726-8000 macfound.org |
|---|---|---|

## Your Legacy

There are over one million nonprofits doing awesome work across our nation. Guess what? Once upon a time they had a founder. When you visit their office and/or website there may be a huge picture of them along with their story of triumph. What will yours be? "What would you like to be remembered for?"

Use your answer as your work ethic and motivation to the legacy you will someday leave behind.

### *Your Retirement Plan*

As the founder of a start-up, you should prepare for your future. No one else will do this for you. No one.

Consider a 403(b) plan for yourself early on.

The IRS defines it as, "As a tax-sheltered annuity (TSA) plan, is a retirement plan for certain employees of public schools, employees of certain tax-exempt organizations, and certain ministers." More information can be found in the IRS Publication 571. *Tax-Sheltered Annuity Plans (403(b) Plans).*

Once you begin obtaining a salary, consult with financial planners who will be happy to come and discuss your options for retirement, as well as how to offer these benefits to your employees. You can also research the US Department of Labor's Employee Benefits Security Administration where they have information on simplified employee pensions available to employers with 100 or fewer employees.

### *Wired For Success: Your Wellness*

A benefit, and a curse, to a founder is your time. You may work long hours, but they are your own. You do not have to clock in. You are an executive and you can work from anywhere in the world.

Although my hours were always non-traditional (more than 40 hours a week), they were mine to make. I abhor clocking in for anyone—a true mindset of an entrepreneur. As a nonprofit leader, I'm available and my creative juices flow at 8 am, as much as they do at 8 pm.

You may be one of those nonprofit founders who may still be clocking in elsewhere. That will change when you become a nonprofit leader. That's something to look forward to.

The plus side is although you may be working on your nonprofit after working somewhere else for 40 hours a week, you are getting yourself used to the long hours you will likely put in at your nonprofit full-time.

I know I have stated it earlier in this book, but I am going to repeat it. You are needed.

"When you do what you love, you will never work a day in your life." It's true as a nonprofit founder and leader.

As you begin to transition to your new position, try to keep your time documented like an employee for legal purposes. You can thank me later should you ever be audited.

I always kept a huge calendar on my office and home desks. Each day, I jotted down when I started and ended my day.

At the end of each payroll period, the hours would be transferred to my timesheet.

One week I worked 103 hours. My assistant thought it was impossible. At the time, I was leading a 24-hour emergency shelter and I spent many days and nights there. From that point on I was dubbed hashtag #nosleep. Staff and board members teased me. They said I was not human. I never felt I worked too much. I enjoyed every second.

Until.

The day of my, first and only (knock on wood), ambulance ride to an emergency room for exhaustion. I thought I was having a heart attack and knew my life was over at the age of 45.

After a night in the hospital I was summoned to bed rest for a week. Then there was that other time where my personal doctor did a "drive-by" to my office. She threatened to call in a bomb scare if I did not leave and go home to rest.

To this day, I have no complaints, but I caution you leading a nonprofit is like a natural aphrodisiac—especially when you are witnessing your hard work paying off. Make sure you know when to stop and take care of yourself. As with so many other entrepreneurs, many nonprofit leaders overlook their own well-being.

It is a reason why in nanpp.org we implemented an area for nonprofit executives called "Professional Recess." We advise all nonprofit leaders to take a break and provide them with the opportunities to do so.

## The "Take Care of You" Tips

**#1:**     Use your vacation time as you have outlined in your employee handbook. Refrain from always eating lunch at your desk. Make sure you hang out with your family and friends. Go home on Christmas Eve! As one board member shared with me one day, "You can't help anyone if you're dead." Yikes!

**#2:**     Never take a pay cut. There may come a day when you question whether you should take a cut in pay. Don't do it. Layoffs may be difficult, but if the going gets tough, remember you were the first employee and should be the last. You cannot stress about your own bills because it will affect your performance to help others.

**#3:** You deserve good office furniture. This may seem like a crazy, or minute thing to cover. However, I am surprised at the number of founders I see working on chairs with stains, or those which looked like they were going to fall apart. Get new furniture. Comfortable furniture for your workspace. Besides the fact you should always be comfortable, you are an executive and will have guests in your office. Guests meaning potential funders. Make an impression.

**#4:** Do not forget your own professional development.

As a nonprofit leader, networking will open the door to opportunities which will help you build and sustain not only the nonprofit but your overall well-being. Join a membership organization with like-minded individuals.

There are many nonprofit membership organizations. The majority represent the "corporation," or the "business of nonprofits," such as the Nonprofit Council. Others represent certain fields such as social workers and grant writers. There are a few for hired (or promoted) executive directors. Only nanpp.org caters to executive directors *and* founders.

NANPP will help you keep up with new trends, resources, and help with connections that will help you grow and expand your nonprofit. Encourage your staff members to utilize their development opportunities so you all can learn how to implement new knowledge and opportunities for your nonprofit. Connect with NANPP online on: Instagram & Facebook: @NonprofitPros Twitter & Linked In: @NonprofitProUSA

You may also be interested in the Forbes Nonprofit Council(forbesnonprofitcouncil.com) as something you can aspire to.

After your organization has over $500,000 in revenues you can apply. The council is an invitation-only organization for senior-level executives in successful nonprofits and the Forbes' name carries weight in business circles.

**#5:** You will be offered a lot of freebies and other donations. It's a good feeling, especially when a program participant or their family gives you something as a thank you. You may be offered tickets to events, free travel to speak at conferences, free clothing, computers, and even money from a funder who may want to control your nonprofit. Accept at your own risk and never use anything for your own personal use which was donated for your program participants. Integrity is everything.

## *Mistakes of Founders*

**#1: Founder's Syndrome.**

It is appropriately defined on Wikipedia.

"Founder's syndrome (also founderitis) is a popular term for difficulty faced by organizations where one or more founders maintain disproportionate power and influence following the effective initial establishment of the project, leading to a wide range of problems for the organization."

Remember you, and/or your board are not the owners.

**#2: Acting Desperate for Money or Resources.**

You will scare people. The only urgency you should ever have to an external party is direct service help to a client who has an urgent need, or your organization is going through an emergency crisis. Request, don't beg.

**#3: Failure to Delegate.** You need to be able to move the organization forward and ensure you own job satisfaction. Try to avoid being too controlling. The nonprofit sector refers to employees who are not in management as "support staff" for a reason.

It is likely because you are the founder, there may be some things you will have more knowledge on. There may be some things you can do better, or even faster than others. Unless, it's urgent, let someone else do it. Engage others.

The spirit of the nonprofit sector is that everyone is valuable. From the maintenance worker to volunteers. Any extra hand, frees up yours to go and move your mission forward. You must trust others are competent enough and may even come up with beneficial ideas you would have never thought of—especially young people.

**#4: Micro-Managing Staff.** If you have the time to watch the details of everyone else, clearly you do not have enough to do. If you hire the right talent, you must trust their judgement and let them soar. Be available to provide guidance.

**#5: Dress the Part.** You're an executive, so you should look like one. You may not have to wear a business suit each day, but business casual is always a good idea. Also keep a business suit, shoes, and if you're a woman—accessories in your office. You never know when a news reporter is going to call to come and do a story or when you are requested to meet with a funder at the last minute.

**#6: Performance Evaluation:** Ask your board to evaluate your performance on an annual basis. You should always be alignment with the expectations of your board. Your evaluation will also help find any deficiencies in your performance. It will also serve as proof that you are not garnering too much influence over the organization.

**#7: Failing to Look for Inspiration Everywhere.** Some of my most amazing moments did not come from people with a ton of degrees or a million Twitter followers. They came from our program participants, the people who lived in our community and even the person who ran the cash register at Staples. Stay open to feedback from others.

## #8: Lack of Organizational Skills

Try and make good use of limited time and organize yourself.

The following are some tools that can assist with you time management. I'm a little bit old fashioned when it comes to time management. I still keep a datebook where I write appointments by hand. Others use technology.

Here are tools you may want to check out.

**Wunderlist.com**: "Organize and share your to-do, work, grocery, movies and household lists."

**Evernote.com**: "Your team can work together, get organized, and collaborate effortlessly on any device."

**Slack.com**: Used by companies such as Airbnb, Capital One, Harvard University, the *LA Times*, Ticketmaster, and others. Their website states, "It's where the people you need, the information you share, and the tools you use come together to get things done."

**Basecamp.com**: "A project management and team communication software for teams."

### *Tricks of the Trade*

### "I Need to Get Board Approval."

People will ask you for favors. You may feel uncomfortable saying no. If you are confronted with challenges which may interrupt the integrity of the organization or program participants, look to your board as the final approval making authority.

### Always make time for the people you serve.

No matter how busy I ever got, whenever a participant needed to speak with me, I made myself available. Some like to put barriers between themselves and the people they help. I am not that type of leader. Never distance yourself from the people you help. Get out from behind your desk and visit your programs and staff. I learned so much by having regular conversations with the people we served and their families. Those were the best days of my job.

**Never put your home address on any documents.**

Remember when you incorporated? If you used your home address, remember to change it to your new physical address or get a PO Box.

**Never bring a client or staff member to your home.**

This may be different for people who live in small towns. However, I have only worked in larger cities. The privacy and security of your family should always be a priority. Everyone should meet you at your office or in a public place.

**Do not follow/friend your staff or board members on social media.**

Keep your personal life separate from your work life. Create business social media handles and let staff and board members follow those. I also did not follow staff, but periodically I did check their social media to ensure they were still a good representative of our organization.

**Use Caution in Your Speech.**

Assume everyone is recording your conversation. During meetings, whether one-on-one or in a group, I would not allow staff to bring in their smart phones. They were also a distraction. This decision was made because one day, an employee shared personal details about a participant after secretly recording our meeting. It harmed and embarrassed them. After the no-cell policy was implemented and updated to our employee handbook.

You should also have well-crafted messages for the media and remember the confidentiality of your participants with reporters as well.

**Be Careful of What You Write in Emails.**

Here are some wise words I once found online. *"Dance like no one is watching; Email like it may one day be read in a deposition."*

In short, do not use your organization email for anything you would not anyone to announce aloud in a courtroom. Also, watch your online postings. In today's world, people will screenshot what you type. Also remember never, ever post anything to any elected official's timeline.

**Never ask staff to request donations from their family or friends**.

They will resent it. Let them know about your fundraising goals and ask them to forward your newsletter or repost on social media.

**Stay Abreast of Industry Trends.**

As a nonprofit leader you owe it to yourself to gain as much knowledge as possible for you, your staff and your board. You can also share these training opportunities when you discuss your organization experience in grant solicitations.

Notable nonprofit publications include: *The Chronicle of Philanthropy*, *The Nonprofit Times* and the *Nonprofit Quarterly*.

These publications are also great places to advertise employment opportunities.

**Meet Socially with Other Founders/Executive Directors.**

For years, I met with another founder, Dawn Murray, who created the House of Dawn.org. We used to spend hours socially venting. We shared issues we could not discuss with our staff, board members, family or friends. Issues only other founders would understand. We encouraged one other. I want to believe we saved each other from going completely insane many days.

More importantly Dawn made me realize the joys of my job.

Trust me there will be days you want to pull your hair out. There will be also be times you will likely stare at your resume and wonder how you can update it. There also may be times you will be so mentally drained, you will wonder if you need a social worker yourself.

No, you're fine.

You just need to find you a Dawn, a David, or a Simone to let it all out and to cheer you on.

# CHAPTER 8
# Board Members

*"The fitting board of directors is less about physical strength,*
*more about mental toughness, with fitting minds and fresh eyes."*
*Pearl Zhu*

Let's play "Nonprofit Jeopardy" (another dream of mines).

Alex Trebek says, "The category is Nonprofit Frustrations." He continues, "Name something, besides money, that raises the stress levels of nonprofit executive directors."

That familiar jeopardy music plays while we write down our answer.

One by one, we all share: "The Board of Directors."

For the first time in Jeopardy history we all win a million dollars because we finally let out a secret we could never share with anyone else.

A little humor, but just know a nonprofit board can be your best friend and ally, or your worst nightmare.

As a founder and/or executive director there is a dichotomy you must quickly understand.

Technically, members of the board are your boss. They provide oversight to what you do.

# Starting & Building an Awesome Nonprofit Organization for a New Generation

On the opposite end of the spectrum, you are responsible for providing them with direction and leadership. There are really no guidelines as to where their oversight stops, and your management begins. Most executive directors are winging it. Most board members are winging it. They just never tell one another.

Many nights, I sat at my desk after a board meeting and asked the question. "Who mentors the mentor?"

As a founder of a nonprofit, you have a little more leverage over the board than one the board has hired. Just a little. That's because you recruited them.

It has been my pleasure to have been exposed to and worked with a wide range of board members. It has been my honor to serve on several boards as well. Their sizes and structures varied. Some were a start-up board filled with family and friends. Another a 40 plus member board with corporate executives, philanthropists and elected officials. Their backgrounds and personalities so vastly different.

You learn to adjust so you can become the centerpiece of your nonprofit like a bouquet of flowers on a table.

There are good boards and there are dysfunctional ones. You, as a leader, should not take anything a board member does personally. They really mean well at the end of the day. Well most of them.

## *Executive Director/Founder on the Board*

Founders and executive directors should not be a voting member on the board. You can be a member, but an ex officio member. If you are a voting member this would be considered a conflict of interest. You will be making decisions that relate to your budget and your salary. Having equal status as a board member is not your role.

Executive directors attend meetings and are involved in the discussions. The board has an option to exclude the executive director in their meetings either through something called an "executive session" or just conducting a meeting without inviting the executive director. That's a red flag for an executive director since the conversation will likely be about them—and not in a good way.

### Board Members are Assets

Your board is extremely important to your nonprofit's success. Your board is legally responsible for keeping you on track with your mission. Ideally, they work to help you secure funding and provide much of the expertise.

Most potential board members are there to help. Your board's executive committee are your partners. Your board chairperson (or president) should be available to attend important meetings with you. They should be willing to speak to the media about the organization. They should be willing to speak with and engage with the people you serve.

Some of the greatest advice I ever received on leadership was from a board member I reported to.

After a grueling day, I shared. He listened to my 15-minute rant and then simply replied, "It's lonely at the top." Gee thanks, but it was factual. He let me know he was not there for my personal meltdown and I've always remembered that.

Most board members are the overseers for the money and the legal obligations of the organization. They have fiduciary and legal responsibility which should not be taken lightly by any founder/executive director. They should fundraise for the nonprofit. They should bring connections that assist you with additional resources.

Board members are not only volunteering their time and expertise to your cause, but they are also putting their professional reputations on the line. If an organization is investigated for any criminal or fiscal malfeasance, members of your board will also be investigated.

Compensation for board members is rare. No payment should be made for their expertise. In the for-profit sector, corporate board members make thousands of dollars. I've been a little jealous of that. Why can't it be the same way in the nonprofit sector where the expertise is needed just as much.

According to BoardSource, "Only about 2 percent of nonprofits compensate board members, and it is unusual outside of large, complex entities such as health care systems or large foundations."

Board service is a volunteer activity and one must be careful about any private benefit to any individuals and conflicts of interest. This also includes hiring any firms where board members have a stake to conduct business on behalf of the nonprofit for payment (self-dealing), making any loans to board members, their family members or private inurement (excessive compensation).

Reasonable expenses for services are permissible (gas reimbursement to board meetings, hotel expenses for board retreats, etc.).

The good news is most nonprofit boards consists of smart and legitimate leadership for nonprofits. Your organization's success or failure will be directly tied to their contribution, or lack of it.

All nonprofits need board members who are raising money, savvy with technology and bring skills sets that you cannot afford to pay salaries for.

In your position, you must know how to keep them happy and engaged. You must remember they are professionals likely employed elsewhere, or have other obligations. They have decided to "serve" because they are aligned with your mission and vision in some way. It is also a way for them to make professional connections and to advance their own careers.

Nonprofit board members should always be revered and respected. You should also never, ever complain about them to your staff, donors, colleagues or program participants. That's disloyalty.

When you need to vent or have a challenge concerning your board, speak with a confidential source such as a nonprofit coach or consultant. Always treat them as a boss, because they are.

# Starting & Building an Awesome Nonprofit Organization for a New Generation

## *Board Recruitment. How Do I Find Them?*

Most nonprofits are always in search of qualified board members. Do not become frustrated if it takes you some time.

As relayed above, many nonprofit boards begin with family members, associates and friends. At some point (as early as possible) you will need to recruit "professional board members."

As soon as you can, try and recruit board members with legal expertise (an attorney), financial (accountant), fundraiser (development), public relations (marketing), IT (computer support), a new media expert, someone with experience working with your program participants and someone who represents the community you are in. You should also try and get someone on your board who has "a name" that will open doors, and checkbooks of wealthy people for you.

Anyone who is recruited for a nonprofit board likely already knows they will be expected to help raise money and/or resources. Do not be afraid to ask if it something they would have an interest in.

### *Board Member Recruitment Resources*
These sites have individuals who are seeking board opportunities.
BoardnetUSA.org|Volunteermatch.org|Boardsource.org|
UnitedWay.org | LinkedIn Board Connect

### *Board Packet and Orientation*
Create a board packet as part of your recruitment efforts. You find samples online, but I prefer to make applications which are in direct alignment with the organization.

This is what you should include:

- Application
- Responsibilities of board members and the amount of their annual board financial contribution.
- Program Information
- Organizational Chart
- Copy of your By-Laws
- Current financial information
- Short questionnaire which asks why they want to join your board.

You should set a yearly goal for board donations prior to them joining. For a start-up a reasonable amount is $1,000-$5,000 a year.

If you have board members who cannot afford to donate personally, they can request donations from their circle of influence. They can create their own special event.

Every board member should be raising money. It is expected and valued by donors, especially foundation representative who will ask about board contributions.

When recruiting board members let them know upfront your financial expectations and supply them with the tools (marketing materials, etc.) necessary.

### Board Roster/Listing

Create a board roster/listing which you will also need for funding requests. Include their name, board title (chairperson, president, member, etc.), profession and terms of service. List the roster on your website. You may be requested to provide contact information for your board. In that case use the organization's address, telephone number and a create an email for the board (board@yourorganization.org).

Never divulge the personal contact information of your board members.

## *Five Tips to Motivate & Engage Board Members*

Each board is unique. There is no cookie-cutter way to engage members. However, as the chief leadership you will set the tone for a newly-created board. Make sure you set the best standards.

**#1:** Let them know they are needed and appreciated.

**#2:** Let them work the room at your events and be sure you introduce them.

**#3:** Purchase business cards for the executive committee (chairperson, president, treasurer and secretary).

**#4:** Stay transparent. Provide them full disclosure of all aspects of the organization (financial, legal, etc.).

**#5:** Hire a consultant or a coach to motivate them.

I have found the best way to get a board member to work is to prepare an assignment with an end date. Instead of waiting for them to volunteer, I always came to a board meeting with an organization "to do" list which had targeted end dates.

I would smile when board members volunteered for projects that fit into their schedules and their line of expertise. After each meeting I would follow-up with them.

You can also develop board committees where board members lead certain aspects of the organization. Typical nonprofit board committees are the executive, development, fiscal, nominating, program and the endowment committees. Excellent information on board committee roles can be found at managementhelp.org.

### Board Meetings

Nonprofit board meetings are not a casual affair. You should always present them in a professional manner. If you find you need to know how to structure a professional meeting, use Robert's Rules of Order as a guideline.

Board members ask a lot of questions and you should always be well prepared.

At each meeting, the board's secretary should take detailed minutes. (Do not be surprised if you are the one taking the minutes in the beginning). After the meeting, they should be sent to all board members. At the next meeting, the minutes should be reviewed and voted on to be accepted.

Board minutes will be needed for submittal with funding requests and government program reports. You will also need them if you are ever audited. Make them succinct and remember not to include any classified information. They are public documents, and anyone can request a copy.

*"I just left a meeting that could have been an email"* is a popular phrase I found one day on someone's social media. It made me laugh. An ideal board meeting is two hours or less.

# Starting & Building an Awesome Nonprofit Organization for a New Generation

Nonprofit leaders should take full advantage of technology for board meetings.

Do you really need to meet in person? Can you utilize video for meetings such as Facetime, Skype for business meetings and GoToMeeting?

For in-person meetings, you should always have great food (hot meals, not just snacks) and refreshments—especially those conducted in the evening after work.

A few days before a board meeting, the secretary of the board should send out a request for board members to add any items to the agenda.

Board members should receive a meeting packet, at least 48 hours before a meeting, which includes the agenda, a copy of the current financials, program and administrative reports.

Management staff (e.g. program directors) should only attend a board meeting maybe once a year to give program reports. Schedule them to discuss their items early on the agenda and when they are done, they should exit the meeting).

### Board Retreats

The only time board members usually meet are around a conference table. That time is used for organization work. The point of a board retreat is to discuss the board, their relationship with one another and to self-assess their leadership. It is also a time to connect socially and share a laugh or two.

Hire a motivating facilitator who can provide you with fun and engaging topics. At the end of the retreat, you all should walk away with goals and action items to make the organization stronger.

Start-ups usually lack the resources to have an out-of-town retreat. In lieu, you can do a one-day retreat at a local venue.

### *Advisory Board: The Board Alternative*

You've found a great board candidate. You have a great interview with them. They are someone you feel would be a great resource. Unfortunately, they have declined joining your full board. They have relayed they simply do not have the time commitment, but they still want to help in some way. Consider creating an advisory board of non-voting members. It's still a win-win for you both.

### *Remember the Good*

My good times with board members have far outweighed any bad times. As a nonprofit leader I have always been thankful for their service.

Nonprofit boards consist of some of the most unselfish people you will likely ever know. They receive little attention or accolades, so whenever you can reward them for their service.

Most of the ones I have ever worked with have been wealthy, had an impressive career and made a difference in the lives of others.

It's a partnership, not a dictatorship on either side. Remember that.

# Starting & Building an Awesome Nonprofit Organization for a New Generation

## *Three Things Board Members Should Know*

**#1:** You have power. Do not abuse it. You should refrain from bullying or micro-managing the executive director and the staff.

**#2:** Your function is not to monitor the day-to-day activities of the organization. You are not the supervisors of staff who report to others in the organization. The only person who reports to you is the executive director. Please do not give the staff directives or assignments and especially if you did not share them with the executive director. A good board does not circumvent the supervisory function of the executive director.

**#3:** Make sure you provide feedback to the executive director annually. Boardsource.org provides excellent, top notch, downloadable tools & templates, as well as webinars on board training.

## CHAPTER 9
# Grants & Fundraising at the Start

*"The secret to fundraising comes down to three magic words: before, more, and strategic." Jay Samit*

A s a nonprofit leader, each and day you should awake with a goal of how to "friendraise" or fundraise to obtain revenue.

Every day. All day. You should devote actual hands-on time to apply for funding opportunities and not only when you have a cash flow shortage.

If you are shy about asking for money or donations, you may be in the wrong business.

Let me dispel the myth most people who are interested in starting a nonprofit believe. Most of your funding will not come from grants. The fact is individuals, like you and me, make up the largest nonprofits donors.

In 2014, the largest source of charitable giving came from individuals at $258.51 billion, or 72% of total giving; followed by foundations ($53.97 billion/15%), bequests ($28.13 billion/8%), and corporations ($17.77 billion/5%).

In 2015, total charitable giving in the US reached more than $373.25 billion shattering records. Of that number 71% were from individuals.[4]

# Starting & Building an Awesome Nonprofit Organization for a New Generation

The absolute first financial donation a nonprofit should receive is from you. The second should be from a board member.

Your first external financial donation will likely come from an individual in what is known as your circle of influence.

Instead of the blanket request such as, "Please donate to our organization." Ask for something tangible and useful.

For example, "Can you help us buy school supplies for ten students?" "Can you donate to allow us to purchase food for our volunteers?" Afterwards be sure and send a thank you letter and publicly acknowledge the gift on your social media. Donors love to see where their money was spent.

After individuals, your next funding will likely come from a grant application you submitted to a foundation or corporation. When you apply you should let them know of the individual contributions already made by you and your board members. Also include any other funding. Very few public funding sources will want to provide a nonprofit's first check.

If you receive $100 from the Big and Mighty Foundation you can use it as leverage. Post it on your website, your social media stating that Big and Mighty Foundation donated to your cause. You do not have to disclose the amount. People usually give when they see others have done so.

Getting a donor management system will help you organize your fundraising. Here are a few with useful tools and product demos. You can take a practice run.

- Raiser's Edge NXT Nonprofit Fundraising Software (blackbaud.com)
- Salesforce (salesforce.com)
- CivCRM (civicrm.org)
- Idealware (idealware.org)

One thing you can learn from the corporate culture is the way they compete for customers. Use the same strategy as you build your funding base to compete for donors. How do corporations do it?

They build a brand.

They educate consumers on their products.

They conduct heavy public relations and valuable customer service.

Use for-profit strategies to fundraise.

Your nonprofit needs to have a diversified funding base which includes private, public funds, and other funding sources to be financially healthy.

## *Successful Revenue Building Strategies From $0*

### *Fund Development Plan*

The is your fundraising business plan with targets on how to meet your funding goals. All aspects of fundraising are included from a fundraisers perspective: individual and major gifts donors, planned giving, grant writing, bequests, capital campaigns, connecting with philanthropists, online campaigns, and special events. As you can see there are many ways to raise funds beside writing a grant.

Your written plan will identify how much you need to raise, from what sources, and how you will do it. It is an investment worth considering early on. You will need to be organized and heavily invested in the fundraising aspect of your nonprofit.

### The Process of the Ask

You should have a standard operating procedure for fundraising that both staff, volunteers and your board members should follow. A script that instructs everyone what information should be shared with external parties.

For example, "This is how we approach a donor." "These are the materials we use for funding requests." "If the media calls, route them to X."

Keep them all in an electronic file which is shareable to your team.

### Restricted vs. Unrestricted Funding

Your nonprofit's funding should not be placed into one pot. Some funding, such as grant funds are "restricted." That means they were donated for a specific purpose, usually program support. Restricted funds may only be used for their designated purposes. No robbing Peter to pay Paul with those funds.

Unrestricted funding (aka general operating support) is funding which can spent where the organization deems appropriate, usually on administrative and operational costs.

Income from your special events are one type of unrestricted funding.

## Online Fundraising/Third-Party Sites

Online fundraising platforms such as donorschoose.org and networkforgood.org can be used as additional resources for donations. They market charities to the public to persuade them to donate to their member nonprofits. They take a small percentage of the funds raised for the service.

Network for Good, founded in 2001 by America Online, Cisco Systems and Yahoo state they have processed over $1 billion dollars in donations since inception.

You can also join AmazonSmile where they donate 0.5% of the purchases to charities selected by customers. Every cent counts.

## Crowdfunding: New Generation Trends for Fundraising

Imagine your mission being shared with millions of people around the world?

That is what crowdfunding does. It is a fundraising source which allows individuals, businesses, and groups to donate to worthy causes or projects. The most well-known is Go Fund Me, which has raised nearly $900 million for worthy causes. Others are crowdrise.org, causes.org, kickstarter.org, globalgiving.org, indiegogo.org. and startsomegood.org.

They really work and are user-friendly.

### *Federated Funds/Employee Giving/ Matching Gift Programs*

This is one of those things they do not tell you in fundraising workshops. Ask your family or friends about possible employee giving programs at their jobs, especially if they work for a large corporation. If they donate to your tax-exempt organization, their company may match it. Many corporations have employee giving (aka workplace giving) programs which are likely done through the HR department.

The two largest employee giving programs are conducted by the United Way and the federal government which is known as the Combined Federal Campaign (CFC). Many nonprofits are accepted.

### *Grant Funding. Who Cuts the Checks?*

There are a trillion books on grant writing. One of my favorites is by Dr. Beverly Browning, CSPF, author of *Grant Writing for Dummies*. Dr. Browning focuses on federal grants which are the most extensive applications to write. It would be wise to snag a copy of her book to assist you.

In my next book, which will be published in 2018, you will be able to learn the "art and the business" of grant writing, so I will not inundate you in this one. For more information visit my website at simonejoye.com and join my e-list to be notified when it is published.

For purposes now, I am introducing you to the "Who's Who" in the grant funding world. It will help you focus on which area you believe would benefit your funding needs the most.

Also, you should know the donor community is a closely-knit network. All people know about them is "they give money." There is so much more to them. If you are going to reach them, you should know who they are.

Check out the Council on Foundations (cof.org) to see what I mean. The Council represents the leading foundation and corporate representatives who support charitable activities across the nation aka "grant makers." They are like a secret society.

One year, I crashed one of their annual conferences for "grantmakers." I was shunned by some because I wanted to be a "grant receiver." I was secretly helped by a few. If I tell you whether I raised funding because of that bold move, I would have to kill you. The point is, as a fundraiser and leader you do what you must do to find the people who cut the checks for worthy causes.

*Corporate Foundations:* This is an area within a corporation where people are appointed to do good work for their product, brand or service. Many of them possess bleeding hearts. I would also imagine the fact their corporation receives tax breaks for donating to charities is also a plus. A corporation will likely not donate to your nonprofit without your tax-exempt Determination Letter in hand.

Corporate foundation executives usually live, work and play in the community you serve. They have a vested interest in its citizens. Their children attend schools there. They shop in the same supermarkets as you do. They want a great quality of life for their employees. They are also the easiest to apply for grant funding.

Their applications are short. This is where a new nonprofit leader should start.

Request a small amount ($2,500-$10,000). You should also look to corporations for day-long volunteer projects. Many corporations give their employees days off to volunteer at charities. They will bring supplies, food and willing hands. I will forever be indebted to AT&T whose employees helped with some major capital projects for our agency. Corporations are also good for asking for product in-kind donations and technical assistance.

You should try and network with them before you make a formal request. Once they give you "anything" you should prominently display their logo on your website. Help drive customers to them and it will also help you get funding and other corporate interest.

**Private Foundations:** According to the Foundation Source, a private foundation is "an independent legal entity set up solely for charitable purposes." The money for these foundations comes from a single individual (e.g., the Bill and Melinda Gates Foundation), or a family (Walmart) foundation.

People who work at private foundations are nonprofit super funding pros. Do not try and pull the wool over their eyes.

Private foundations are created to help make the world a better place. They know the issues. They know the impact. They know nonprofit leaders. They make it their business to invest wisely in sustainable programs and they do it diligently. They are also the

ones who will visit your organization on "site visits" before they ever issue a check.

If you do not get funding from them at first, one thing is for sure, they will love giving you advice. They may even tell you what other foundation may be interested in funding your cause. Pick up the phone and talk to them.

Foundations can give large donations to nonprofits, but they are more likely looking for "partnership" opportunities.

***Family Foundations***: Also considered a private foundation. The staff are usually a wealthy person's relative or trustee. They can be very snobbish, but approachable. Their funding likely hails from individuals who have left a personal financial legacy (e.g. the Rockefeller Foundation). My favorite is the Arthur Blank Family Foundation in Atlanta. In 2016, they distributed $22 million dollars to worthy causes. If you're lucky enough to meet one of their representatives, without an invitation, it will probably be at a conference or in the home of one of your wealthy friends.

***Community Foundations:*** These foundations include financial and investment advisors, banks & trust companies that serve the philanthropic sector. They are some of the greatest financial minds who pool the assets of donors to invest and support charities in their local communities.

SunTrust Wealth Management is one to research. If you are in one of their communities, you should consider applying. However, your appointment will likely be scheduled a year later.

# Starting & Building an Awesome Nonprofit Organization for a New Generation

***Government Funders:*** Government funding are taxpayer funds which are distributed through legislation. Due to their large amounts which are usually given for several years, they are considered the crème de la crème for grant funding. They are highly competitive because you are competing against national or statewide nonprofits. There are also local government funds, but they are not as large as the federal and state grants most of the time.

In exchange for government funding, you will be assigned a program officer who will monitor every eraser you purchase. They will write to you let you know you forgot to put a period at the end of a sentence in one of the progress reports you must send in to receive payment. Meanwhile, you're sitting around wondering how you will make payroll with a payment delay.

Government funds are sometimes difficult to plan for. There are some nonprofits who will not even apply for government funding because of the stringent terms.

Many religious organizations avoid them because of the separation of "church and state." Government funding does not support religious activity and they will not allow you to "purchase" things such as that building or van you may need.

As a new nonprofit, you should work your way up to apply for government funding. Try to start with local or state funding opportunities before you apply for federal funding.

You can view federal government grant opportunities at grants.gov.

## *Low-Cost Start-Up Funding Ideas*

### *Special Events*

This area of fundraising can generate a lot of revenue for your organization. There are tons of events you can put together without much up-front costs including online events.

Events are not just for building revenue. They are also a way to recruit volunteers and showcase the work that you do. Eventbrite.com is an excellent source to post events and may even help you get new people involved in your organization.

***Become a Fiscal Sponsor/Agent.*** After you get your 501(c)3, join the Fiscal Directory.org as a fiscal sponsor/agent and help another new nonprofit. In the beginning we charged a $100 application fee and a 3-5% administrative fee.

***Fee-Based Services.*** Are there services you can provide that others will pay for? Goodwill Industries has an excellent model. They get donations of clothing and re-sell them. By doing so they fund their nonprofit and provide employment to those in need.

Also, after you create that great logo, create T-shirts, hats, mugs, tote bags, etc. and sell them on your website.

### *Sponsorships*

***Corporations*** follow the for-profit model. Sponsorships are usually given from the marketing departments. Their staff are hired to make money for the corporation, unlike the foundation people. You will need to approach them differently.

They are mainly interested in large events that garner hundreds or thousands of people. You are competing with large events so do not waste a lot of time in this area if you cannot provide the numbers or have a personal relationship established.

**Local Businesses** are a great source to request support from. You may obtain hundreds of dollars in unrestricted revenue. Ask everyone for support. From the supermarket manager to the lawn care company. Remind them their donation is tax-deductible. They will likely also want a tax break for their business. Why not give them one through your nonprofit?

### Cryptocurrency

Is this the new form of funding opportunities? It does present a new and exciting alternative to traditional donations according to cryptcoinnews.com.

Cryptocurrency is a decentralized digital currency you can sell for real money. Overall the transactions are anonymous which may be an appeal to some who already donate in this manner to nonprofits.

Examples are Bitcoin, Coinbase or Ehtereum.

You may not have yet noticed, but there are already signs up in retail stores that accept cryptocurrency.

Cryptocurrency is growing fast in commerce, technology and the banking industry.

SuperPacs are accepting them as donations. United Way Worldwide, Khan Academy and Greenpeace accept them from donors.

There are no payment processing fees for donations, so nonprofits get nearly 100% of donations. Research and see if this is something which will help you raise funds.

### Building a Millennial Donor Base

The nonprofit sector is only beginning to understand millennials as donors. Most have not managed to successfully incorporate them into their fundraising plans.

Millennials, those who are now in their 20s and early 30s, make up around 80 million people in the United States. The Foundation Center reports, "Members of the millennial generation account for $200 billion in direct purchasing power and they are set to be the beneficiaries of a $41 trillion transfer of wealth from older generations."

They are the generation who have a larger global mindset and a greater sense of social responsibility.

Young people in their 20s and early 30s give differently to nonprofits than other generations. Millennials are the online generation. Mobile technology and social media is an intricate part of their daily life.

If you want to reach millennials, you will not need to go through other sources such as a foundation. You can go directly to them on social media. In turn, they will give on your website. They also are more likely to give smaller amounts monthly than one large payment.

They are the generation that wants to share and brag on social media to their friends about their causes. Use that to spread your message and gain even more donors.

Consider creating a young adult advisory board for fundraising.

You will be ahead of your counterparts.

# CHAPTER 10
# New Generation Marketing and Communications

*"I've learned that people will forget what you said, people will forget what you did, but people will never forget how you made them feel." Maya Angelou*

Y ou are a start-up nonprofit. You will need people to learn about your services and the work you do. You want everyone to spread the word about your nonprofit with their friends, family and colleagues. You will want people to feel what you do. Talk to the heart and the head will listen, is what I always believe.

A good marketing strategy will build your reputation and allow you to compete with other nonprofits, even the veteran ones.

Connecting people to your nonprofit is all about telling your story. It's about crafting and distributing messages.

Publicity means support.

Here are some suggestions to get your marketing and communications plan off the ground.

**#1: *Create a Slogan*** and a hashtag about your nonprofit's services and your advocacy message. Ours was the name of our organization, #youngpeoplematter, which was created years before other #matter hashtags.

Another one of my favorites is a simple, yet effective message: #LiveUnited which is the slogan for United Way.

### #2: *Target Your Audience.*

Ask yourself, "Who am I trying to reach?" Is it new funders? New program participants? New partners? Once you determine your audience, create segmented marketing campaigns with different messages designed for them.

### #3: *Create Eye-Catching Printed Materials*

Start with your stationary/letterhead and email signature. Every person affiliated with your organization should use the same format, colors, fonts, etc. Keep everything in conformity as this will help identify your brand and keep your professional appearance.

On your email signature, add your logo, website link, along with social media icons and links. On your stationary, list all the names of your board of directors and advisory board members on the left side margin. Place your name and title on the bottom left.

Brochures, flyers and your business cards should be "charitable-friendly." Include lots of pictures of real people, statistics and your organization's impact. Fact Sheets about your programs are also great and will go handy with your grant applications.

Keep in mind the adage of the marketing world, which is still true today, less (words) is more.

Create Infographics which are "graphic visual representations of information, data or knowledge intended to present information quickly and clearly." You should design a few for your services and outcomes that "pop" out at your readers.

My favorite site for creating Infographics, and other graphical masterpieces right now is Canva.com. This book cover was done using Canva. It took me about 20 minutes. Canva has templates which allow you to become your own graphic designer in no time. It's amazing what you can do there for free.

Creating infographics is also great assignment for an intern or a volunteer who wants to assist with marketing and promotion.

***Make a Newsletter.***

A one-page electronic newsletter should be sent monthly. Share stories about program participants and make an ask for support. Add a button so readers can easily forward to others.

Each year, you should circulate at least four newsletters especially during the year-end holidays when people give the most to nonprofits. Great sources for sending our mass emails is Constant Contact (free for charities) and Mail Chimp.

***Craft an Annual Report.***

In the for-profit world this is a publication which is presented by public corporations to their shareholders. The report denotes the company's financial condition and operations for the preceding year.

Nonprofits also use annual reports to highlight their mission, vision, impact. It is also another way to tell your story, attract donors and other supporters. More nonprofits are going paperless with their annual reports and displaying them on their websites.

You can also consider making yours into a video or a slideshow. Check out annual reports of other organizations and get creative with your own.

### #4: *Press and Publicity.*

With every accomplishment (e.g., new board member, special event, participant story, new funding, etc.) send out a press release to the media, making use of radio and television reporters. The more publicity you get, the more you are proving you are legitimate charity doing great things.

Search online for distribution companies which offer to send out press releases for free.

### #5: *Your Website.*

It goes without saying that your nonprofit should have a website. It is important that you display exciting and useful information, along with a highlighted area where donors can easily click to donate.

Here is some information to consider for your nonprofit website:

- Organization's leadership (staff and positions)
- Mission and Vision statements.
- "Contact Us" with the full physical address of your organization.

- Programs, service and accomplishments.
- Testimonies from program participants (videos would be a plus).
- Press releases, videos and any media coverage.
- A listing of all supporters, donors and partnerships/collaborations; and, if needed, event listings and a volunteer sign-up information page.
- Other resources and referral information for your program participants.

Weebly.com offers a great place for free and low-cost professional websites, as well as Citymax.com. You will also be able to purchase your company's e-mail account which you should do as soon as you get your domain name.

If you can, set up automatic payments for your domain name renewal. There is nothing worse than learning your website is down, or your email was rejected because you forgot to renew your domain. You never want to be offline because that just may be the day someone tried to donate that million dollars you have been waiting for.

### #6: *Billboards.*

A very effective form which are surprisingly not that expensive. I have used them in the past to get messages out to young people. CBS Advertising gave us a heavy discount for a six-month run. Our ads appeared on trains, buses and in neighborhoods where we knew young people congregated. Our purpose was to get young people to come to our agency. We did not expect the large amount of in-kind donations and financial support the billboards also garnered.

### #7: *Create an App.*

Apps are a great way to raise money and get donors to share information. They are handy and convenient. Apps are expensive, so you may want to try and get someone to make one as a donation. When I did research, the lowest cost I found was $5,000 for a basic app.

You can consider promoting an app that already exists by another organization that aligns with your mission. For example, a safety app by your municipal government for emergency evacuations. Reach out and let them you would like to partner with them for promotional purposes.

### #8: *Visual Storytelling.*

We live in a video crazed world. Power the leverage they bring to getting your message out. Try and go viral.

Make short 60 second or less "commercials" with program participants at random and post. You can even create slideshows and turn them into videos right from a smartphone. Create a two-minute video for your organization people can view on your website.

Set up a Google for Nonprofits account, (G Suite for Nonprofits). Once that is done you will be able to enroll in the YouTube for Nonprofits Program. As a nonprofit, you will get, "access to unique YouTube features to help connect with supporters, volunteers, and donors." Remember to use your logo as your avatar.

My favorite part of the program is where you can get production access to shoot or edit your videos at YouTube's studio in Los Angeles, New York, and a host of international cities at no cost. Go YouTube!

**#9: *Quick Response Code (QSR)*.** How about a barcode for your nonprofit like retailers use for products? You can add them to your printed materials (business cards and brochures).

Share information such as your social media pages, a link to a donation page, collect email addresses, or provide directions to your agency.

In China, they have gone straight from paper currency to QSR codes, bypassing credit cards and debit cards, for monetary collection. Your nonprofit can do the same.

**#10: *Create a Widget.*** A widget is a shortcut icon which allows you to launch an app. Do you know those countdown clocks on a website? That's a widget.

Widgets are great for embedding codes into your website like event registration forms and other things which require you to obtain personalized information.

Also, WordPress (another great place to create a website) has some good ones.

**#11: Photo Storage.** Create a Flickr.com account to store all your photos. You will appreciate having your organization's pictures handy all in one place.

## Social Media: Put a Face on It.

Use your social media to build your brand, advocate for your cause, recruit volunteers, promote your staff, and let potential program participants know the services you provide. You should post messages every day. If you do not have time to post separately on each social media outlet, Hootsuite and Sproutsocial allow you to do it all at once for a fee.

Use social media to reach out to celebrities.

## The Day Tyler Perry Showed Up

One of the most successful individual giving campaigns I have ever spearheaded was done for two reasons. One, we urgently needed $45,000 to keep our doors open. Two, I wanted to merge social and traditional media as a financial appeal. It was something I had been longing to do despite the naysayers, including my board, who said it would not work.

It was a now or never type of thing that paid off.

Speaking to gatekeepers and making appointments does not abode well when a nonprofit is having a fiscal crisis. In a nonprofit's lifetime, there will be that word crisis you will may find yourself in. It's not just for your program participants.

Here's what worked for us.

Our participants made a list of their favorite celebrities. We then took our appeal to Twitter. Meanwhile, I sent out press releases to our local media. Two of the major network local television news stations visited and did great stories.

One morning after one of them ran our story, we received a telephone call directly from media mogul, Tyler Perry. Within the hour he was at our door—without any bodyguards or assistants. He came alone and spent time speaking to our participants. They took selfies and he changed their lives.

One of our participants said, "I can't believe you are here."

Mr. Perry responded, "I don't know why not, you have been tweeting me every day. Then I saw your executive director on the news this morning…"

Before he left he graciously donated the $45,000 we needed. Ironically, it was the weekend of his 45th birthday.

How long did it take?

Exactly two weeks.

Besides the gratefulness of Mr. Perry's donation and presence, which kept our doors open, it leveraged an additional $15,000 in donations from others within a few days.

The merging of major media and social media with celebrity appeals should not be overlooked as you build your nonprofit. Never let anyone deter you from your ideas even if no one has ever done it before.

### *Social Media Special Features for Nonprofits*

Many social media companies support nonprofits and the good work we do each day. That's a plus and will make getting out your message easier. Here are a few which may be helpful to you.

- Facebook allows nonprofit to develop fundraising campaigns.
- On Twitter you can create online petitions and even conduct a Twitter chat.
- SnapChat allows you to create short temporary videos. It is also an excellent way to reach teens and young adults.
- You should also consider Google+ and create an organization page on LinkedIn.

### *Purchase Tables at Events*

Buy that ticket, or reach out to organizations for a scholarship to attend nonprofit conferences. Purchase a table which are usually reasonable. Look for events that will put you directly in front of potential funding sources and other potential partners. You want to be in the rooms with people who will help you take the nonprofit, and your career, to the next level. The cost of the table may be a wise investment to get you where you need to go faster.

If you are not able to purchase a table, but can still attend, consider putting your marketing materials on a USB flash drive to give out when you hand someone your business card.

### *Get Out From Behind Your Desk*

You are the not the Wizard in the Wizard of Oz. Get out of your office and move around with program participants and staff. Visit your program sites. Talk to your staff & volunteers. As a leader you should always want to connect with those who benefit from your work.

In a few short years, I created the largest street outreach for homeless youth in Atlanta. I want to believe we managed to do so, because I walked the streets and we went further into the communities than any other nonprofit. I was told I should be scared to go into abandoned buildings. My board relayed that was not something an executive director does.

At the end of the day, I decided what I wanted to do to help more. There was nothing more fulfilling than me connecting with those kids on the streets. It gave a boost to my staff and volunteers. It kept me wanting to work even harder to end homelessness among our young people. Due to those efforts we garnered more media coverage and ultimately, more donations which allowed us to save more young people.

Even when I led a large organization, I conducted monthly "town hall" meetings at our three program sites to make sure I was in touch with the families and the kids we served.

Honestly, I would have preferred to be the head of the street outreach team, rather than the executive director on many days. That is how passionate I was. No one may not be able to understand your passion, but you.

Make the time to connect and get out of that office.

---

# CHAPTER 11
# Consultants

*"Many people are not ready to pay for advice they can use, so the
few that do, break boundaries and soar higher."*
*Bernard Kelvin Clive*

As a start-up, you will need someone who possesses knowledge that likely does not yet exist within your organization. You will need someone who can assist with those lingering feelings of self-doubt that may cross your path.

No matter how much experience you or your team have, an external objective viewpoint will provide you with an outlook you may have missed.

A consultant also saves you money from hiring a staff person and paying fringe benefits.

Balance is everything. You may soar in one area and are average in another. Everyone has an area to excel.

### You Will Need the Help

I have never had to find a consultant. They have always found me. I am sure they will find you as well once you begin your public relations. A funder may even suggest one to you.

Even as a consultant myself, I still hired others.

I'm a firm believer everyone has a lane in this world. I do not know everything, and I do not expect everyone to volunteer their services. There are talented people who should receive compensation for that talent.

As a founder, I just did not have the time to set up our fiscal management software. I hired a consultant who set up our QuickBooks perfectly for about $1,500. That system was used for years and was an excellent investment. I hired another to set up our HR files and to advise me on labor laws. Because of their help, I focused more on fundraising and other internal processes to successfully grow the nonprofit.

The best consultants to hire are those who have had hands-on experience. I would not hire a realtor to find me a house who rented an apartment. That's just me.

Hire a CPA to help with fiscal matters, a HR expert for personnel and labor matters, or someone like me an ex-executive director, development director for your administrative and fundraising needs.

## Most Sought-After Nonprofit Consultants

Nonprofits leaders use consultants for a myriad of areas. There is no shortage for their services.

Almost each position in a nonprofit can be done by a consultant, including the executive director. I believe the most sought after are grant writers and other types of fundraisers, program evaluators and those who specialize in board development. In today's nonprofit, you will also need a media/public relations consultant to give you an edge.

## Grant Writer: Can We Pay Them from the Grant?

The answer is no. The entire profession frowns upon it.

Grant writers will likely tell you that is the "most asked" question in their profession.

Writing grants takes a highly specialized expertise. A grant writer spends hours on writing, researching, developing/enhancing your program or organizational ideas to properly present to funders. They also create budgets, evaluations, set up partnerships, and provide technical assistance to you and your team which ultimately makes your organization stronger. You also become a more viable candidate for funding.

There is never a guarantee you will obtain grant funding, even with the best written application. There are a multitude of reasons your nonprofit may be denied. Your financials may be shoddy. You may be duplicating services, or the donor just does not have enough money for all their requests.

What happens to that unfunded grant request you paid a grant writer to produce? Many feel they have wasted their money or were somehow robbed. Nothing could be further than the truth.

Assuming it was properly written, you now have information to use for other grant requests and your organization's marketing materials. My work has been used repeatedly to obtain grant funding from other sources, of which I have never received any additional compensation.

There is also this fact, grant writers have an uncanny ability to "speak to funders" while adhering to strict deadlines, tedious application upload processes, and the additional expenses involved: travel time, mileage costs, emails, telephone calls, photocopies, etc. Ask yourself, would you do all this work if someone promised to pay you in the future?

I tell potential clients when you invest in a grant writer, it is like hiring an attorney. As a legal client, you will likely pay an attorney fee whether they obtain an innocent or guilty verdict for you. Why? Because attorneys have done the work for your case. It's the same with a grant writer.

In addition, you are taking a chance with donor trust. Most funding sources will not give you funds to pay a grant writer. An experienced grant writer knows this and will not allow you to pay them on contingency.

If you are somehow awarded funding and pay a grant writer from program funding, you have lied to the funder. You have also taken funds away from services to your program participants. That's bad nonprofit leadership.

To save costs, you should consider drafting a grant request on your own and then hire a grant writer to possibly edit or proofread it which is more cost-effective than creating a grant proposal from scratch.

### *How Do I Determine What to Pay a Consultant?*

A nonprofit consultant will usually let you know of their rates which are done by the hour or per project. The average range is $75-$175 per hour for smaller nonprofits and $250 per hour for larger ones.

You can negotiate a fair price by researching the salary for the position you are hiring them for.

According to salary.com, the median annual salary for a grant writer is $66,647. Divide $66,647 by 52 weeks for a weekly salary of $1,281 per week/40 hours per week=$32.04 per hour. That amount can be used for payment negotiations.

### *Proper Reporting for a Consultant*

At the end of the year, you must provide all consultants, who earned over $600, with a IRS Form 1099 MISC which is generated through your payroll processing service when your W-2s are distributed to employees.

Never hire anyone to work "off the books" of your nonprofit organization. Make sure you receive a sample contract outlining their services, the billable rate, along with an invoice for services.

When you hire a consultant make sure they complete a IRS W-9 form with a valid social security, or EIN number.

---

# CHAPTER 12
# 12 Things I Wish I Knew at Start-Up

---

*"When the game starts, you don't really look at uniforms."*
*Billy Butler*

Hindsight is always 20/20.

When I look back there are many things I would have done differently when I began a nonprofit, or took the helm of one.

Perhaps they will be helpful to you on your journey.

***I Would Have:***

#### #1: **Not Brought Work Home.**

When I left my office, I would have stopped working unless there was an emergency.

#### #2: **Been Selective about Attending Events.**

I would have let someone else attend programming oriented conferences, events and training sessions. I would have only focused on the once geared specifically for all nonprofit employees. I would also not have attended so many technical assistance workshops for government funding. Most of the information they will post on their websites. If they require mandatory attendance, send someone else to represent your nonprofit.

## #3: Invested in a Coach Early.

Eighty-six percent of for-profit companies use them to sharpen the skills of high-potential leaders. It took me and my board of directors two years to get our nonprofit administrative and operational structure to a professional level.

During those two years, I was drained and discouraged more times than I could count. It felt like I was in a desert. I yearned for honest feedback. Most people, such as your staff and board, may agree to everything you say. They are called "the yes people."

You need people who can give you honest and frank feedback. I also wished I would have included a plan for group coaching for my team, including the board.

Everyone could use a cheerleader. If I had a nonprofit coach from the beginning, I believe their energy and encouragement would have helped me focus better.

## #4: Created a Better Plan for Fiscal Emergencies

There will likely come a time in your nonprofit life cycle where you are worried about meeting your payroll, paying your bills or experience a cash flow shortage.

No, let me change that. There WILL come a time when this will happen. I am almost certain of it.

Here are three ways to research emergency funding "before" you need it.

- Ask your bank for a line of credit as soon as you are credit worthy. Likely year two or three, but not in your first year.

- Apply for nonprofit loan funds with foundations.
- Find resources which provide "nonprofit bridge funding."

**#5: Been Better Prepared for External Economic Risks**

I wish we would have thought about how to stabilize operations when affected by a government shutdown or a national recession which reduced a large amount of individual donations one year.

**#6:      Opened a Retirement Fund for Myself**

**#7:      Created Exit Strategies for Changes in Board and Executive Leadership**

**#8:      Purchased Property for the Nonprofit rather than Leasing**

**#9:      Not Stressed over having Audited Financial Statements done**

Until your organization earns over $500,000 in revenue save costs and do not let anyone talk you into spending thousands of dollars to prepare an audited financial statement. If you can get it done pro bono by an accounting firm, that's wonderful. Otherwise, do not worry yourself.

You can have a Financial Review or a Financial Compilation by an independent auditor. A review and compilation are a good gauge of the nonprofit's financial health. Even more, funding sources will accept them and/or your 990 in lieu of an audited financial statement. Just point out that you are a small nonprofit.

If you need to have an audited financial statement done, I strongly recommend a using a Certified Public Accountant (CPA) who is familiar with the Generally Accepted Accounting Principles (GAPP) and nonprofit accounting standards.

## #10: Utilized the Bank's Business Perks

One huge mistake I made early on as a founder was not taking advantage of all the benefits available with a business checking account, including better interest-bearing accounts. The bank representative never mentioned them when I opened the accounts.

Make sure you inquire about special programs for nonprofits "and" small businesses. For example, you get to use the business line for deposits, get reduced rates on credit cards for your nonprofit, free overdraft protection, etc.

Also, you want to make sure you have a direct telephone number for a bank representative. Use it to begin to establish a relationship. In the future, you should ask them for a line of credit, a credit card and a financial donation.

## #11: Made Strategic Planning a Continuous Model

It's your first-year anniversary. You are in the zone and your nonprofit is doing well, helping people, raising funds and making alliances. What's next?

I wish I knew how important a properly crafted strategic plan is critical to the continued growth of a nonprofit. It will help you develop efficient operations and good support systems. Your programs will become more sustainable.

A strategic plan helps you identify where the organization is headed and will help you make any necessary program or administrative modifications.

**#12: Used all my Personal & Vacation Days.**

# Conclusion

Thank you for reading!

Hopefully, you feel empowered and are on your way to starting and building an awesome nonprofit organization for a new generation.

As you have learned by reading this book there are many facets to a nonprofit.

With the tools I have shared, I hope you will go forth and help hundreds, or even thousands, of people.

The work you are inspired to do is transformative. Remember that. There can be nothing but goodness ahead for you.

Begin to be thankful for the countless gifts and blessings you will receive because of your unselfishness to help humanity.

I cannot tell you how proud I am of the seeds I have sown which have reaped harvests for countless others.

It is truly a blessing to be a blessing.

However, as you have read, everything that is gold does not glisten. Ignore the hate. Ignore the ones who will be ungrateful of your service and sacrifice. Ignore anyone who may not celebrate your differences or your lifestyle.

Most of them will not have the courage to start a business in their lifetime. The others have never helped anyone but themselves. They too have a place in the world. Try your best to keep them out of yours.

# Simone Joye Eford

You have no time for them because there are 11 million other nonprofit professionals ready to welcome you and learn about what you do.

Never forget the people who will come to rely on your work and leadership. The ones who you are likely starting and building your nonprofit for. Remember you are their champion among other nonprofit influencers and stakeholders. Making their lives, as well as your own more meaningful, should keep you strong and your walk steadfast.

Immediately after I completed this book, I began working on the next book in this series. It will be an in-depth, no holds barred, inside look at the art and business of grant writing. Look out for it in the spring of 2018. I hope you will use it as another resource for your library as well.

In the interim, I would love to learn about your nonprofit and how you are utilizing what you may have learned from this book.

Congratulations in advance on your many accomplishments to come.

Yours in service,

*Simone Joye Eford*

More info: SimoneJoye.com
Socially: @SimoneJoyeEford

> *Please consider leaving a book review on the site where you obtained a copy.*

References

[1] "Charity Officials Are Increasingly Receiving Million Dollar Paydays." Andrea Fuller. *Wall St Journal*. March 6, 2017.

[2] Public Disclosure and Availability of Exempt Organizations Returns and Applications: Documents Subject to Public Disclosurehttps://www.irs.gov/charities-non-profits/public-disclosure-and-availability-of-exempt-organizations-returns-and-applications-documents-subject-to-public-disclosure

[3] "Nonprofits Hungry for New Leadership." Sacha Pfeiffer. *Boston Globe*. May 18, 2015 https://www.bostonglobe.com/business/2015/05/17/nonprofitretirements/QkFp8drbL4YsMExtwlGnuJ/story.html

[4] "Giving USA 2016: The Annual Report on Philanthropy for the Year 2015" Giving USA. June 13, 2016